Matt —

After years of procrastination, a li[ttle]
goal-setting finally got the book written.
How much can I write off? ^_^ Enjoy the read —

JR Bailey
June '07

The Parental Peace Accord

Jack L. Bailey, J.D.

Bloomington, IN   Milton Keynes, UK

authorHOUSE®

AuthorHouse™
1663 Liberty Drive, Suite 200
Bloomington, IN 47403
www.authorhouse.com
Phone: 1-800-839-8640

AuthorHouse™ UK Ltd.
500 Avebury Boulevard
Central Milton Keynes, MK9 2BE
www.authorhouse.co.uk
Phone: 08001974150

The information in this book is not intended as legal advice. The law changes
frequently and varies from jurisdiction to jurisdiction. It is important for you to
seek legal counsel from an attorney licensed to practice law in your jurisdiction.

First published by AuthorHouse 5/7/2007

Library of Congress Control Number: 2007901178
ISBN: 978-1-4259-9629-1 (sc)
ISBN: 978-1-4259-9628-4 (hc)

The Strategic Coach and The R-Factor Question are registered
trademarks of The Strategic Coach, Inc. All rights reserved. Used
with written permission. www.strategiccoach.com.

Printed in the United States of America
Bloomington, Indiana

This book is printed on acid-free paper.

DEDICATION

To my wonderful sons, Ross and Bryan; and Joan, a great parenting partner.

ACKNOWLEDGMENTS

This book was prompted by a life of experiences and observations; some childhood, some personal, some professional, some wonderful, and some ugly. What made the book a reality was the influence of some very significant people in my life.

First and foremost, I want to thank my family. My sons, Ross and Bryan, are the joys of my life and my best friends. Their mother, Joan, is one of the most giving women I know, and I am fortunate to have her for a parenting partner.

I want to thank Patty Moore, my friend and faithful paralegal, who sat through hundreds of divorce client appointments, often hearing the same story, over and over again. It was Patty who would always tell me that I should put the non-legal, commonsense advice on a video or in a book. I finally took Patty's advice. She's a wonderful woman and an incredible mother.

I also have to thank Dan Sullivan and the great staff at The Strategic Coach®. The tools and concepts they have armed me with have provided a powerful impact on every part of my life. I especially want to recognize Lee Brower for getting me on track and providing me with the tools to create a strategic plan to make this book a reality. Likewise, I want to acknowledge the guys in my Goal Cultivator Community. If I hadn't had to answer to them, this book may have never gotten finished.

I am grateful to Dave LaRue, my friend, my mentor, and my coach. Although he lives in God's country, any time I'm in need of some quick motivation, he is always just a phone call away. He has a natural ability to always see the bigger picture, and he knows just how to share that picture with everyone else. I'm fortunate to know him, and I'm blessed to have him as a friend.

I also owe a huge debt of gratitude to Judy Noble for giving me encouragement, support, and advice when I needed it the most. She knew when to push and when not to push. She is also extremely bright, and it was wonderful to have her editing assistance. More importantly, her daughters are fortunate to have a mother that is such a strong role model.

I would never forgive myself if I didn't acknowledge my great friends and business partners, Mike Watkins and Dale Field. Mike is a soul mate who also had a pretty rough childhood and used that experience to be successful. Dale is a master of details and follow-through. Without him I don't think anything would ever get done in our companies. The three of us have been friends and business partners for years, and although we haven't always agreed on everything, I don't think we have ever had a cross word between us. Not many can say that.

Most of all, I want to recognize the children. Of all people, it is the children in our world that have influenced this book the most. Every time I see a baby or young child, I am overwhelmed by the innocence you can see in his or her face. That innocence is a constant reminder that they are entitled to feel loved and have a fun and happy childhood. It is a constant reminder that we, as adults, have an obligation to put them first. It is a reminder that it's not about us—it's about the children.

CONTENTS

1 | AN INTRODUCTION

This book is not a divorce guide. It is also not a book on child psychology. Instead, it is a book about parents utilizing a unique process to achieve a truce during and after their divorce for the benefit of their children. There are tons of books available to help parents get through the psychological trauma of divorce. There are just as many works to be found offering advice on how to deal with children who have been unable to adjust to the dissolution of their parents' marriage. This is not one of those books.

Hopefully, the contents of these pages will help reduce the need for some of the aforementioned treatises. Too many times the focus is on the children *after* the damage has been done. There is a reason for this. Divorcing parents are often so wrapped up in their own emotional turmoil—which partially consists of concern for their children—that they really don't have the time, strength, or insight to be an effective support system for their kids. Their faulty assumption is that after the divorce is over and the dust settles, the kids will automatically adjust. If you're lucky, maybe that will happen. In most cases, very little occurs with children automatically.

The best parents can hope for is to try to anticipate their children's concerns and issues *before* they become damaging. This is the tricky part because no two children are going to have the same anxieties. The differences are caused by a myriad of variables, such as age, confidence, maturity, support systems, and interpersonal skills. Hence, there is no strict blueprint to follow that dictates the exact procedure to ensure well-balanced children who are experiencing a parental divorce.

This book subscribes to the belief that the best person to identify and address the specific and individual needs of the child is the parent. It is the parent who should know the child better than anybody. It is the parent who should be in the best position to anticipate the concerns of his or her own children. It is the parent who is going to have the best opportunity to address the child's issues before those issues grow to damaging proportions. Lastly, it is the parent who holds a place of trust with the child and has a better chance of keeping the doors of communication open.

There are many books that have been written by learned psychologists, psychiatrists, therapists, and other health-care professionals, all of whom have impressive degrees and designations after their names. There are other books that have been written by parents who have had first-hand experience with their own marriage dissolution and the effects it had on their children. Some of those parents have felt the need to share those experiences so that others can learn from them, while others have shared their experiences as a part of their own personal closure process.

I am not a psychologist. I am not a psychiatrist or clinical therapist. Nor do I profess to be a great sage who holds the secrets to smooth dissolutions and stable children. I am a lawyer who has handled hundreds of divorce cases and witnessed many rights and wrongs in the way parents have handled issues facing themselves and their children in a dissolution setting. I am a divorced father who has been blessed with special relationships with my children and ex-wife. I am an orphan who has spent the precious time of childhood in orphanages and foster homes. I am a child born out of wedlock who never met or saw my biological parents. I am an adopted child who was never allowed to grow close to my adopted parents. Lastly, like everybody else, I am a product of my childhood, my society, my experience, my mistakes, my values, and my conscience.

Throughout my years of private practice, I have seen good people who were totally unaware of what was happening to their children during the turmoil and emotional traumas brought about by their divorce. I have sat in my chair of professional "objectivity" and watched in horror as parents have allowed their children to become the unnecessary victims of a necessary divorce. I have "fired" myself from divorce cases when my stomach could take no more of the neglect or misconduct of my own client toward his or her children.

Call me naïve, but I believe the vast majority of parents truly love their children and would do anything for them. It just gets a little complicated when you can no longer live with the person who helped you bring them into the world. Emotions are out of control, perspective is lost, and it becomes very difficult to stay grounded and remember what is really important.

In 2001, there were more than a million divorces in the United States. In 1997, one out of every two first marriages ended in divorce, and 60 percent of second marriages ended in divorce. Since then, those numbers have remained pretty consistent. And yes, children are affected. The U.S. Census Bureau reports that 28 percent of those homes with children have single parents as heads of households. According to the Statistical Abstract of the United States, since 1972, each year over one million American children have seen their parents divorce.

Accordingly, an awful lot of children become victims of divorce. But it doesn't have to be that way. If parents can muster the strength to pull themselves away from the emotional turmoil long enough to get a glimpse of reality and perspective, their children can not only survive a divorce, but can also be strong, well-adjusted kids with the opportunity to lead fun and balanced lifestyles. To accomplish this, each parent must dig deep into the love that they have for their children and find the power to create a truce. The *New Webster's Dictionary of the English Language* defines the word *accord* as an "agreement; harmony of the minds," hence, the name of this book, *The Parental Peace Accord*.

The Parental Peace Accord is not some magic gimmick that will make your kids okay with your divorce. It does not represent some cutesy trend like the latest diet fad. Plain and simple, it is work. It is a unique process that provides an approach for parents to achieve some harmony for the benefit of their children during the dissolution of their marriage. If you care enough about your children to have this truce, to create a parental peace accord with your ex-spouse or soon-to-be ex-spouse, you had better be committed to working harder than you ever have before.

If you could talk to great political leaders like Ronald Reagan, who worked hard to end the cold war, or Jimmy Carter, who facilitated the Camp David Peace Accord, they would tell you that those results were achieved through an awful lot of work. It required flexibility. It required concessions. It required tolerance and patience. And most of all, it required an enormous amount of time and commitment.

So the question is, my friend, are you willing to do all of this for your children? Don't say yes too quickly. If you are truly committed to having success with *The Parental Peace Accord*, you and your child's other parent are going to have to do things that other divorced people say are crazy. You will be doing things that will cause people to say, "By God, that's just not natural!" And yes, you will be in public places with your children, and possibly your ex, and in your peripheral vision, you will see people leaning close to each other and whispering. And if you've got the right perspective, you'll say to yourself, "Screw 'em, I don't care what they think, this is about my kids, not them!"

Now this is where you've got to trust me. If you keep your head on straight, and really make some emotional stretches, in the end those same whispering idiots will be coming up to you and saying, "You know, I just want you to know how neat I think your kids are. They are just so well-adjusted and balanced. You guys have done a great job." When you hear that, and you will, you will feel a warm glow that only a parent with a deep abiding love for their children can feel.

So what am I talking about? What is it that people will find so weird that it will make them whisper behind your back? Well, I promise not to dwell too much in this book on just *my* personal experiences, but I have had a few that can certainly shed some insight on what I'm talking about. So here are some things that people saw between my ex-spouse and me during the fourteen years after our divorce and before our kids went to college.

People saw both of us at our children's sporting events and music concerts, sometimes actually sitting together! Why, can you imagine the rumors? There were times during some of these events people saw us laughing and being quite cordial with each other. That certainly made people talk. And what about those times people saw us actually *talking* to our ex's significant other? Now that's just weird! Or how about the time that about one hundred guests showed up at my house for my son's high school graduation open house, only to find out my ex was there and had prepared all of the food in *my* kitchen. Why, these people are just way over the top!

Okay, my commentary on these events may be a little sarcastic, but it is true that people just don't know how to react when they see a divorced couple getting along so well. Now before you jump to the conclusion that we were different than most divorcing couples, let me assure you it wasn't always that way.

My ex and I had our fair share of shouting matches, tears, throwing things, door slamming, swearing, and just about anything else you can think of outside of physical abuse. There was a time she probably had more anger for me than anyone else in her entire life. There was a time when I thought she was so crazy she needed to be committed. If you had told either one of us at that time that we could have a civil working relationship, we both would have told you that you were crazy, right after we told you to go to hell!

But we both got past it, and here's how. In the middle of our divorce and after one of our worst late night fights, we stopped and looked at each other in complete physical and emotional exhaustion. It was at that point that we saw how ridiculous our arguments had become. It was at that point that we realized there was something a lot more important upstairs, hopefully asleep. It was at that point that we came to the agreement that every decision we made from then on would be based on what was best for our two children. It was at that point that we created our own personal parental peace accord.

From that point forward, every decision became a lot easier. We had a great house with lots of equity and low payments. I had the greater earning capacity, and it wouldn't have been right for our children to see their Mom in an apartment and paying more in rent than the existing house payment. She gets the house; it's best for the children, so I had to buy another house. I found one nearby that I really didn't like, but it is close enough that the kids would be able to ride their bikes back and forth. I bought a house I didn't like because it was best for the kids. We threw out the court's holiday visitation schedule because our respective families had traditions that were important to maintain for our children. Do you start to see the pattern here?

Is any of this easy? Hell no. You have to exercise tolerance. You have to force yourself to look the other way sometimes and keep your mouth shut. You have to give in once in awhile. You have to be willing eat a little crow at times. And what's the hardest part? Communicating.

You probably weren't doing a great deal of communicating before the divorce. Well, now it's a whole new game. If you're going to do the right thing and be there for your children, you and your ex will be communicating about everything. You will have to keep each other informed about school work, report cards, dentist appointments, sporting events, dances, proms, holiday plans, vacation plans, discipline issues; the list goes on and on.

You may as well get used to the fact that this type of communication is going to be very tough in the beginning. This will be a new area for both of you, and it is not going to be easy. Emotional wounds will still be raw and not communicating would certainly be a lot less painful. If communicating face to face or on the phone is too stressful or uncomfortable, then get creative. Communicate by e-mail or voice mail. Just figure out some way that the two of you can have civil communications regarding your children without antagonizing the other. As hard as it may be, try to be nice. It's a start.

I can make you one promise. As tough as it will be in the beginning to have these communications, if you are committed to it and work hard at it, it will get easier as the years roll by. You just have to figure out what works best for the two of you. If you have to start with e-mails, then do it. But be careful. E-mails are cold, and it is very difficult to express inflections, and this can lead to misinterpretations.

Voice mails have the advantage of allowing inflections to be heard, but they are still another form of one-way communication. What I really hate is when parents put notes for each other in the child's backpack or luggage. All this does is put the child in the middle of parental communications. I think children of divorced parents deserve a little better than becoming carrier pigeons for their parents. But if that's the only way the two of you can figure out to communicate, then so be it, as I suppose it is better than no communication at all.

The point of all of this is that you have to be willing to communicate regardless of how difficult or uncomfortable it may seem. We're talking about your children. They are worth communication efforts on your part. If you aren't willing to communicate, then throw this book away or give it to someone else because you don't have what it takes to engage in the unique process of a parental peace accord for your children.

Yes, I've heard it before. "*I'm* willing to communicate, but *she* is impossible and will never engage in a civil conversation." Fine, then you need to proceed with one-way, civil communications for the benefit of your children. If your ex comes around, great. If not, then you still did the right thing for your children.

The Parental Peace Accord is a unique process designed specifically for the benefit of your children and results in an agreement. An agreement takes two parties. If both parties aren't willing to communicate, then there can be no agreement. If that's the case, then there is a real lack of perspective as to what is important in your life. Your child has a right to have happy childhood memories and you have an obligation as a parent to help create those memories. You and your spouse are getting or have gotten divorced, not your children. In all likelihood, they still love you both and are really caught in the middle.

You can get out of each others lives as spouses, but not as parents. The children are still there and always will be. It is important for you to take on the perspective that the love you have for your children is the one common denominator between you and your ex-spouse, all emotions aside. It is that one common denominator that can allow you and your ex to form a post-dissolution partnership for the benefit of your children. Like it or not, you both have an obligation to your children to be or become parenting partners.

We enter into partnerships and agreements every day. There are business partnerships created to make money. There are consumer agreements, for example, that say "If you fix my car, I'll give you money." There are emotional commitments that say, "If you need me, I'll always be here for you." So doesn't it make sense that we would be willing to enter into a partnership or agreement for the sole benefit of our children? You are at a time in your life when it is extremely important for you to take a gut check on what is important as it relates to your children.

How many times have we heard parents say, or said ourselves, "I would give my life for my children." What a huge statement of love and commitment! And most parents who make that statement mean it quite literally. They would make their body a human shield to protect their child from impending danger. They would give up a vital organ if it meant continued life for their child.

So if you've made that statement or feel that way, committing yourself to participate in *The Parental Peace Accord* is a pretty small price to pay. Sure, you may have to deal with someone you can't stand or someone who has hurt you beyond comprehension. Yes, you may have to put yourself in some pretty uncomfortable situations. But if we're talking about your children, that's a lot easier than taking a bullet or giving up a life-sustaining organ.

If you're feeling challenged right now, good. You're going to find out whether the love for your children that you have always talked about is real or just talk. You see, I didn't write this book for you or your ex-spouse. I wrote it for your children. I've made it a fairly short, easy read because I know you've got a lot going on right now, and I want you to finish reading it. I didn't use a lot of my long legalese terms or post-graduate vocabulary because I want you to grasp the concept regardless of whether you are a ditch digger or a nuclear scientist. I even made the title and cover pretty inconspicuous for the self-conscious. So now you get to find out what you're really made of and what is really important in your life.

Thus far, you could be having any number of reactions. You might be saying this Bailey character is crazy as a loon. You might be thinking I live in a fantasy land. Or maybe you're scared silly. Whatever you're feeling, I encourage you to let it go. Let the love that you have for your children give you the strength to make a stretch and do some things you didn't think you would ever be able to do. Let that parental love fuel your commitment to work hard and do whatever it takes to give your children the happy childhood they deserve.

At the end of each chapter in this book there is a page for you to jot down any notes or thoughts that you may have as you read this book. I encourage you to do so because there is a pretty good chance some things are going to hit home. In writing this book, my perspective is colored by my experiences as a parent, a child, and an attorney. People actually pay attorneys like me enormous hourly rates to hear what is not legal advice, but some good old objective common sense. So you got off easy with what you paid for this book. Trust me; your attorney won't be upset because there are really other things he or she would rather be discussing while earning their hourly rate.

So, are you in? Are you ready to read the rest of this book with an open mind? Are you ready to set aside your emotions and focus totally on your children, not yourself? Are you willing to accept that some things on these pages will work for your circumstances, some won't, and others are worth a try? Are you ready to open a different set of communications with your parenting partner that at times will feel awkward, at best? Are you ready to work harder on this than probably anything you ever have before? And lastly, are your children worth doing all of these things?

If you've answered every one of these questions with a *yes*, then at least one half of the equation is willing. We will address the other half, which your ex represents, throughout the rest of this book. But right now, it's time to get to work. It's time to start changing the way you have been thinking. It's time to get the focus of your children's happiness as the common denominator between you and your parenting partner. It's time for you to do your part in creating your own parental peace accord.

Notes and Thoughts

_____

_____

_____

_____

_____

_____

_____

_____

_____

_____

_____

_____

_____

_____

_____

_____

_____

_____

_____

_____

_____

_____

_____

_____

_____

_____

_____

_____

_____

_____

_____

_____

_____

_____

_____

_____

_____

_____

_____

_____

_____

_____

_____

_____

_____

_____

_____

_____

2 | PUTTING EVERYTHING INTO PERSPECTIVE

I really need to make an important point here before you read any further. There are times in this book that it will seem as though I am promoting and encouraging divorce. Nothing could be farther from the truth. I believe in marriage and have deep admiration for those loving couples that have spent the better part of their lives together. However, this book is being written on the assumption that you have already divorced or made the decision to divorce or you wouldn't be reading it in the first place. More importantly, if you made that decision, this book is written to try to reduce the chance of your children becoming casualties of divorce. It just doesn't have to be that way.

Okay. Let's get started. Right now there is a pretty good chance that you're feeling about as low and torn apart as possible. Then again, maybe not. People have as many different reactions to divorce as there are reasons for divorce. Suffice it to say, those reasons are endless. Maybe you're one of those people who are thrilled, feeling that a two-ton weight has been lifted from your shoulders because things are finally out in the open, and you can start to move on. Perhaps you're one of those who are feeling excitement at the prospect of starting a new life with a clean page. Conversely, maybe you're experiencing feelings of disconnect and confusion. Or is it guilt, anger, remorse, fear, betrayal, shame, panic, or regret? Or maybe you just don't know what the hell it is you're feeling. It's okay. Whatever it is you're feeling, it's probably pretty natural. As I said earlier, we are all products of our environments. The environments that lead us to divorce are all different, so it's only natural that our reactions are going to be different.

Happy Days Of Marriage

Although the outcomes may be different, most of us probably started out the same way. We met that person that made our heart beat just a little faster. When you heard the phone ring, you were just hoping it was him. When she walked into a room, you felt like the lights got brighter. And when you got married, you felt pretty sure you were the luckiest person on the planet.

Then the two of you did what married people do. You got that first apartment or house together and set up housekeeping as a couple. Pretty cool stuff. Sure, she made you move the furniture twenty times before it was just right. And he would have never gotten those pictures on the wall right without your supervision. But it was all fun. Little things, like the first time you grilled out at your new home, became events.

If you're in the majority, just when you thought life couldn't get any better, it did get better. You were told you were going to become a parent. A baby! Now that made you stop and think, didn't it? I'm going to be a father! I'm going to be a mother! What an exhilarating feeling. There were lots of things to think about. We have to keep "Mom" healthy. We've got to get the "baby's room" done. Who's the best pediatrician? Which is better, breast milk or formula? Yes, there were a lot of important issues to be addressed. But addressed they were, one by one, by two people who were committed to making the very best decisions for their child.

Now here's a day you won't forget—the day you saw your child for the first time. We all remember looking at that tiny, little, innocent face. We can't forget those tiny hands and feet or the softness of our newborn's skin. And as we looked at that little infant for the first time, we felt the wonderment of having brought a living human being into the world. And later, some of us experienced that again. And maybe again.

Many of us got to enjoy a lot of firsts together. These were milestones that everybody we knew heard about. That first step was a bigger event than the Super Bowl. That first dance recital was more memorable than a Broadway play. That first home run ranked right up there with the accomplishments of Babe Ruth. Yes, we made Kodak a lot of money.

So what happened? Was it boredom? Was it unfaithfulness? Was it money, job stress, child stress, bad sex, no sex, or were you just victims of modern marital statistics? Sorry, you're reading the wrong book. There are a lot of books and health professionals out there that may help you save your marriage. And if you honestly believe your marriage can be saved, put this book down and get to work on that immediately. Just remember, there needs to be two of you that believe your marriage can be saved. Don't confuse denial with the potential for your marriage to be saved.

A spouse's denial of marriage failure reminds me of a case I heard in Indianapolis back in the late eighties. Indiana is a no-fault divorce state. This means that a spouse wanting a divorce need only allege that there has been an "irretrievable breakdown of the marriage." The courts consider the mere fact that things are bad enough that one party has filed for a divorce a pretty good indication that there has been an irretrievable breakdown of the marriage. As I was waiting in the courtroom for one of my cases to be called, I heard an elderly attorney arguing on behalf of her client that there had NOT been an irretrievable breakdown of the marriage. She went on to argue that the judge should dismiss the Petition for Dissolution filed by her client's spouse and order these two to work out their differences. While the attorney's argument may have had some good old-fashioned moral merit, the judge was astonished by the argument and denied the request.

So how do you know if the marriage is over? Well, some would say, you just know. Usually when I've had a divorce client in my law firm, I could pretty much tell whether the marriage was over, or whether it was going to be one of those filings of a Petition for Dissolution of Marriage that had a good chance of being dismissed later as a result of reconciliation by the parties.

For instance, if I have a client in my office who is exhibiting a lot of emotion, such as anger, regret, or pain, I know there is a chance that the parties might still reconcile after they go through some of that initial emotional roller coaster. However, if I have a client that is very non-emotional, indifferent, and resigned to the fact that the dissolution is going to take place, it is very probable that a dissolution is going to occur. Typically, this client has already gone through the arguments, the tears, and high emotions, only to come to the conclusion that a divorce is best for everybody. But these decisions don't always come easy.

Staying In It For The Children

Without a doubt, it is the concern and welfare of our children that can make the decision to dissolve a marriage the toughest. For most of us, our children are the most important priority in our lives, and the last thing we want to do is anything that will jeopardize the level of stability in their lives. Unfortunately, many of us know couples who are very unhappy and have elected to stay in the marriage "for the sake of the children." We have also seen those same couples divorce the minute the kids are grown or off to college.

Right or wrong? Well, first of all, there is no right or wrong answer that provides an ironclad rule for every situation. If clear heads prevail, the parents themselves are the best ones to determine what is right or wrong for their children. But there are things to consider.

I've seen couples in a relationship that has deteriorated to the point that they are totally miserable and can't stand to be around each other. These same couples will often be the ones that will engage in hostile arguments with little provocation. Some of those arguments escalate to physical outbursts which involve throwing things or, even worse, physical abuse.

At the other end of the spectrum are the couples that have shut down so much that they hardly even communicate. They live in their own cold, separate worlds, serving their time until their sentence of punishment is over. That imprisonment may end with divorce when the children are grown or through the inevitable death of one of the parties.

So you have to ask yourself, is this really in the best interest of my children? Is it in my child's best interest to see his or her parents in vicious or physical arguments? Is it in my child's best interest to grow up with parents who are unhappy and very cold toward each other? And lastly, is it in my child's best interest to grow up in an environment where the parents are stressed, tense, or walking on eggshells?

Trust me, you can find volumes of studies that relate failures in marriage to the parties being products of what they witnessed as children. Children with cold, unaffectionate parents may grow up to be cold and unaffectionate spouses. Children who grow up witnessing physical abuse as a way of life, may often become abusers themselves. If I'm striking a chord here, and you're ready to throw this book away, let me make one more point. There are also studies that show many children grow up to be the opposite of what they witnessed with their parents. Those with cold, unaffectionate parents may grow up to be warm, loving spouses, just as those who grew up watching the horrors of abuse are committed that they shall never be like that. These children will often become adults who declare, "My children will never feel what I felt as a child."

I'm one of those products. Some of my formative years were in an orphanage, and I felt very lonely and unloved. When I was about nine years old, I remember watching all the grandparents and relatives coming to visit the other children during a Sunday afternoon visitation period. As I sat in the corner feeling jealous and very sorry for myself because there was nobody there to visit me, I thought to myself, "If I ever have kids, they will never feel like I do right now."

All I can tell you is that my sons, both of which are now young adults, and I are extremely physically and verbally affectionate to each other. If they come home from college, or visit, or call on the telephone, the last words we invariably say to each other are "I love you." I can honestly say that my sons, although their parents divorced, have never felt the way their father did at the age of nine.

So what does all this mean? It means that you as a parent are in the best position to know if staying in your marriage for your children is the right thing to do. Not an easy decision, but nobody said being a parent was going to be easy. There are a lot of factors to consider. What are your children witnessing in your current marital relationship, and does it set a good example for them? What are the ages of the children? Is it a first marriage or have they already been through one divorce? Is the current environment emotionally healthy for them?

Yes, a tough decision indeed! But deep in your heart you know the answer. And guess what? Your children, if they're old enough, know the answer too. I can't tell you how many times I have inquired of divorcing parents as to how the children are taking it, only to be told that the child's response was "Well, it's about time… you guys are miserable." Our kids are smarter than we give them credit for. We may think we have them fooled in our effort to protect them, but the fact is they usually already have it figured out.

Life Is Short

So here you are, walking around like one of those comic strip characters with a bunch of question marks floating around your head. You've taken an objective look at your marriage, as best you can under the circumstances, and have come to the conclusion that the marital relationship isn't good for you or your children. But you still have this anxiety about the whole divorce thing and putting the children through it. It seems like it might be easier to not make a decision and maybe just put off the inevitable.

The fact is you have already made a decision. It's just a little difficult to act on it because not acting on it is the path of least resistance. This is not uncommon, especially when a person has reached that point of indifference and resignation that we discussed earlier. If the marriage still has a chance, all of the emotional charges of hurt, anger, and resentment are keeping you busy. But if it's over, and you're at that point, then prolonging the inevitable is just making you miserable, and there's a chance you're making your children miserable too.

If that's your current situation, I have to tell you, life is just too short to live that way. You're missing out on precious quality time you and your children can spend together. You've heard the old saying. There *is* life after divorce. And if things have gotten to the point that you have to get out of your marriage, that life after divorce is a whole lot better for you and your children. Regardless of your child's age, he or she will be grown and gone before you know it. The fun and quality times with your children should be a priority, and you have more control over that than they do.

Undoubtedly, if you're at the front end of the divorce process, there are a lot of issues ahead, such as custody, child support, visitation, and housing. All of these will be addressed in other chapters. The focus of this discussion is to not let the sand slide through the timer of your child's life while procrastination toward the marital relationship develops into apathy.

In the worse-case scenario, I have seen this approach have some tragic results. Parents continue to live in a state of flux and tension. Much like those old pressure cookers we remember, eventually something has got to give. I've seen this happen to very responsible parents, and it isn't pretty.

Years ago, I represented a very classy, educated, professional woman who was married to a well-respected physician. They were living an emotional nightmare because although they both knew the marriage was over, they just couldn't bring themselves to start the dissolution process. One night during an escalated and heated argument, her emotions got the better of her, and she slapped her husband across the face. Before he could even think, he instinctively slapped her back. They stood looking at each other in horror that it had come to this, only to be devastated when they turned and saw that their seven-year-old daughter had gotten out of bed and witnessed the whole thing.

Fortunately, this case had a happy ending. The parents were so shocked by the occurrence that it served as a wake-up call for them to realize what was happening and where they were heading. From that point forward all of their focus was on their little girl and her well-being.

They filed a <u>Joint</u> Petition for Dissolution of Marriage as a symbol of their commitment to work together in doing what was best for their daughter. From that point forward, the dissolution proceeding was uneventful, and they have a very relaxed, friendly relationship, with their daughter as the common bond. More importantly, their daughter is the benefactor of that bond, as she has a loving relationship with both of them. The last I heard, the parents were working together in planning their daughter's wedding, and all three family members were looking forward to that happy occasion.

For some, the wake-up call has been worse. Picture the stay-at-home mother who would not get out of a terrible marriage because she didn't know how she could support herself and still be able to stay at home to care for her children whom she loved dearly. The tension and stress continued to build day by day, week by week. Finally the pressure cooker blew. In a moment of irrational emotion, she shook her three-month-old baby boy because he wouldn't stop crying. The child died of shaken baby syndrome, and the mother was sentenced to serve time in prison. A prison not nearly as bad as the permanent emotional scarring caused by knowing that her fear of leaving a terrible marriage took her child and resulted in a tragedy far worse than any financial hardship. It is also sad because such tragedies are not uncommon. How many times have we opened the paper or listened to the news to learn of a spouse committing murder or suicide during the course of a failed marriage or divorce?

These horrible stories are not for shock value. They are true. And in most cases, the parents involved never saw it coming. It's also a pretty sure bet that the parents involved all knew deep in their heart that the marriage was over. Whether they were in denial or whether they lacked the fortitude to make tough decisions becomes insignificant in light of the tragic results.

If you can't bring yourself to do what you know is right or if you don't think you can muster the strength to make those tough decisions, here's a different approach. Use the love you have for your children as a source of strength. The physical and emotional stamina exhibited by parents who are protecting the well-being of their children is amazing. We've heard about parents who have done seemingly impossible feats, like lifting a car, to save their child. We've heard of parents who have given their lives to protect their children. Yes, parental love can be a powerful force when channeled in the right way for the benefit of our children.

So instead of focusing on your emotions of hurt, anger, or resentment, shift the focus to your children. What are their emotions? What are they witnessing between their parents? How much of your own emotional energy do you have left for them in your current situation? Are they old enough or observant enough to have already figured out what you dread to face?

This is a time when your child needs you to have perspective. Yes, we all had hopes of having that perfect marriage and wonderful relationship that lasted "till death do us part." But the truth is, it just doesn't always work out that way. In fact, the statistics in today's society indicate there is a pretty high chance it won't work out the way we had intended when we took that trip down the aisle.

But as a parent, you can't just say, "Oh well, I guess that's the way it goes; the statistics were right." No, you have a responsibility to get your child through this situation. That child has a right to feel loved and be happy. If you make that your focus, everything else will fall into its proper perspective.

Notes and Thoughts

_____

_____

_____

_____

_____

_____

_____

_____

_____

_____

_____

_____

_____

_____

_____

_____

_____

_____

_____

_____

_____

_____

_____

_____

_____

_____

_____

_____

_____

3 | BREAKING THE NEWS

Probably one of the most stressful events in a divorce is breaking the news to our children whom we love so much. Here we have spent our lives committed to protecting them from all the wrongs of the world, only to be the bearer of news that will have a significant impact on their lives. This is probably the most critical time for them in the divorce process, and it is imperative that it be done with forethought and planning.

Again, the variables for this undertaking are endless due to factors such as the child's age, the environment up until that time, the number of children, the circumstances of the divorce, and the personalities of the children and the parents. Hopefully, you are the best person to know how this should be handled because you know your child better than anybody. But then again, perhaps with all of the emotional turmoil you've been going through, you might not be totally on your game as a parent.

So while there are not any black-and-white answers or formulas to address this stressful subject with your children, there are some general, common sense guidelines, which you might want to follow. The most important thing to do when considering these guidelines is to step out of your shoes and into those of your child. Imagine receiving the news from their perspective. Think about the least stressful way for them to hear this news and what can be done to make them feel secure.

I always recommend that parents consider a "who, what, when and where" approach to this difficult task. This approach does a couple of things. First, it makes the parents think about what they are doing. Secondly, it results in a plan of action to be followed for the benefit of the child. This is about the child, not you. This is where *The Parental Peace Accord* takes its first active role in letting the decision of how things are handled be determined by what is best for the child. So what do we need to consider?

Who?

First of all, this is not a contest between the parents as to who would be better at broaching the subject or who is closer to the children or who is the most tactful. Often in the midst of a divorce, it is natural for parents to become adversarial and to consider everything in a win/loss perspective. Get rid of that perspective. It will never serve you, your children, or your parental peace accord well.

If parents want to do what is best for their children, the ideal approach would be for both Mom and Dad to be there to discuss this significant event in their children's lives. This will send a lot of strong subconscious messages to your child. It will tell him or her that although Mom and Dad can't live together, they are very much together when it comes to things affecting him or her. It will eliminate the danger that the absent parent automatically be dubbed the "bad" person.

Additionally, if both parents are there, it gives the child more places to go for comfort and support. In most cases, your child loves both of you very much, notwithstanding how you may feel about each other. You are not a Petitioner and a Respondent to your children. You are Mommy and Daddy regardless of their age. Even if your child saw it coming, there is still the impact of "this is really going to happen," and they need to have as many support systems available as possible.

Lastly, if both parents are there, they can provide a support system for each other. This is one of the toughest things you will ever have to do. Hopefully, you will find yourself and your soon-to-be ex on the same team. You will both be trying to give your child comfort and support. Each of you may be overcome with your own emotions during this discussion, and it will be good to have the other there to take the "tag-team" handoff and continue a discussion of reassurance for your child.

Okay, so much for ideal situations. There are certainly going to be those circumstances where both parents can't be there. Dad's in jail. Mom ran off with another man—never to be heard from again. Your spouse is an alcoholic and can't stay sober long enough to have a discussion with your child, or anybody else for that matter. Or your spouse is abusive and can't come around without violating a court order. Unfortunately, these scenarios present themselves quite often.

If you have to do this job by yourself, forget for the moment why you're having to do it by yourself. Your spouse isn't the issue here; your child is the main focus. On the positive side, if it is impossible for your spouse to be there for reasons like those mentioned above, there is a pretty good chance your child won't be blindsided by the news of your divorce.

As you go solo on this task, remember one very important thing. Regardless of how terrible you may think your spouse is or how terrible they actually may be, your spouse is still your child's Mom or Dad. While it may not seem like it right now, there is a bond between your child and *both* parents that is so strong it overlooks the very worst in people.

As a child, when I was in the orphanage in Orange County, California, I was amazed by how much some of the kids loved and missed the very parents who had caused them to be there in the first place. On visitation days, I would see children of alcoholics running with tears in their eyes to the parent that had been deemed unfit by the courts. I remember kids who spoke fondly of their parents that were serving time in the California penal system. And that magical bond between parents and children works both ways. Think of the times have we seen the parent of a mass murderer being interviewed on television say something like, "In his heart, he really is a very sweet and good boy."

So you may be married to a drunk, an inmate, a cheater, or an absolute derelict, but that person is still your child's parent, and you would be wise to remember that when breaking the news of your upcoming divorce. Again, the best way to avoid this pitfall is to focus on your child during the discussion, not your spouse. Let your child know that even if your spouse isn't there, you know if circumstances were different, he or she would want to be there. (Remember that part in Chapter One about doing tough things and eating a little crow?) Keep the discussion focused on reassuring your child about what he or she is feeling as opposed to why your spouse isn't there.

What?

What do you say? If you're reading this section in hopes of finding a script, you're going to be disappointed. Once again, there are just too many variables to have a one-size-fits-all approach to these matters. For instance, your child's age will have a huge influence on how and what they are told. You certainly talk differently to a child at the tender age of four than you do your seventeen-year-old teenager.

It's a pretty good bet that a four year old is not going to understand the term *divorce*. With a child that age, a more simplistic approach, such as, "Mommy and Daddy love you very much, but we just can't live together anymore," is going to be more effective. You must then go on to reassure the child that Mommy and Daddy will always be there for him or her and that mommies and daddies never stop loving their children.

Regardless of the child's age, there is one habit that I strongly encourage; try to begin each statement with a positive message. If you can develop this habit, it will soften the emotional blow and will probably keep things civil between you and your soon-to-be-ex-spouse. Notice that the statement I referenced above for the young child begins with "Mommy and Daddy love you very much…" Statements beginning with, "You are very special to us," "we will always be here for you" and "we are so blessed to have a child like you come from our marriage" are very positive and reassuring, even if followed by a less than cheerful subject matter. Listen to me very carefully: You *cannot* say these things enough to your child.

For the older teenage child, a different approach is required. The last thing in the world you want to have happen is for your child to feel you are talking down to them. Talk to them with a parent's love and compassion, but talk to them as an adult. Be responsive to their emotions, but give them credit for having a brain. They may have seen this coming long before you did!

Most importantly, with an older teenager, be frank and honest. Tell them, "This is the hardest thing I have ever had to do" or "You're pretty smart and insightful, so perhaps you saw this coming before I did..." Your teenager will appreciate and respect the fact that you are talking to them like an adult as opposed to a little kid. However, just because they preferred to be talked to like an adult, don't forget they are still young, and they now have to deal with some very life-altering news. They need you more than ever, even if they don't admit or verbalize this.

Whether your child is a toddler, an adolescent, a teenager, or an adult, there is one constant. They need to know they are loved. They need to know that you will always be there for them. They need to know that the failure of your marriage was not their fault. They need to know that they still have two parents. It is your job as a parent to continually send these messages. Your marriage may be on the rocks and your spousal relationship coming to an end, but your parent-child relationship will go on for a lifetime. Your obligation as a parent is to help your children through this in the present and in the future. Whether you are dealing with current dissolution issues or issues down the road, such as a wedding or grandchildren, your responsibility is to lessen the negative impact of all of these on your children.

When?

Yes, I know, there is no good time to tell the children. But there can be some psychological advantages to good timing. Certainly, the worst timing would be to tell your child after he has already heard it from someone else. Let there be no mistake, children should only learn of their parents' divorce from their parents. For them to hear it any other way is negligent at best, cruel at worst.

Although it is not easy, the earlier the children are in the loop the better. Everybody will be going through huge periods of emotional adjustment, and this gives them more time to adapt to this new circumstance. Your children will also not feel as though they were the last to know, after the grandparents, your minister, friends of the family, etc.

I'm so obsessed with the well-being of children that I even think there is a better time of week than another. I encourage parents to have this discussion with the children on a Saturday morning. Why so specific? Because if the conversation is held in the morning it gives you the rest of the day to be around your children and observe how they are dealing with the cards they have just been dealt. It gives you a chance to be there for them when they may very well need you the most. You have the weekend to spend with them, allowing them to get some kind of grasp on the situation before they go to school on Monday morning and before you go to work.

I also have a lot of reservations about telling children in the evening. Kids are like adults in that they sometimes do most of their in-depth thinking when they're laying awake in bed. I think parents should think twice before telling their daughter, "Mommy and Daddy are getting divorced, but we love you, everything's going to be all right, now run along to bed." Picture the child lying in bed staring at the darkened ceiling with all the fears, sorrows and anxieties in the world bearing down on him or her. This is not the supportive way to handle things. You can only be supportive if you are there and 100 percent present. That's hard to do if your child has gone to bed, and you're still at the kitchen table wondering if that went all right.

Where?

Okay, so we know we're going to broach this subject in the morning when we have a lot of time ahead of us to be there for our child, preferably the entire weekend at least. But where is the appropriate place to undertake this heart-wrenching deed? Well, excuse me, but you're an idiot if you're thinking of a crowded public place. This is not television. This is your child. Inviting them to lunch or dinner at a great restaurant for this serious conversation may work on those soap operas, but this is real life.

If you're in a public place, you have probably just placed restrictions on your child's right to react in an honest and normal manner. Children are very self-conscious, and it is very unlikely that they would bare their souls and true emotions in a public place. If your child can't be sincere and spontaneous in their reaction, how can you be effectively supportive of him or her?

The best place is probably right at home—a place of security and familiar surroundings. It is a place that gives the child grounding in a big, unpredictable world. It is a place of comfort and family support. Your child can be completely uninhibited is his or her own home, and that is the type of environment he or she needs for you to get a good read on your child's true reaction and emotional state of mind.

When deciding where you can have this discussion with your child, remember the foundation on which *The Parental Peace Accord* is based; it's about the child, not you. The decision of where to have this discussion should have nothing to do with your work schedule or what fits best with your plans. The only consideration to be made is, "What will make this easier for my child?"

Reactions Of Your Child

Just as all children are different, so will be their reactions. Some will be shocked, some reduced to tears, some angry, some passive, some withdrawn, and a few will be happy. You're job is to be supportive. Don't try to manipulate your child's emotions. Allow them to be expressed.

Most of all, just listen. If you're fortunate enough that your child is expressing their feelings to you, whatever you do, don't interrupt them. Even if you don't agree with what they are saying, or even if you feel they are being unfair, they need to be allowed to get their emotions off their chests. It's about them, not you.

After they have finished expressing themselves, acknowledge their feelings. If you dismiss their feelings as misguided or inappropriate, it is unlikely they will be inclined to share with you again. If you think their feelings are truly valid, then let them know that. This is a time where they need support and validation.

On the other hand, you may have a child that makes no attempt to express himself, which leaves you totally clueless as to how he is feeling. It may be that they need some time to let this news sink in. That's okay. Now, aren't you glad you've got the whole weekend ahead of you to monitor this situation? Give them time. Let them process at their own speed. It's reasonable to ask some gentle, open-ended questions, but don't force the issue. It's okay to say, "I know this is difficult, and I want you to know I'm here for you if you want to talk."

This is a time to tell your child how much you love him. Be honest and tell him that by breaking this news you are experiencing every parent's worst nightmare. Let him know you both love him, will always love him, and will always be there for him. What you say is so important because your child will remember this dialogue for the rest of his life.

If your older teenager isn't talking, it forces you to walk a fine line. On one hand, you don't want to pressure her or force a dialogue. On the other, you don't want to turn your back with the assumption that when she's ready to talk, she'll let me know. If a day or two passes without meaningful conversation, go back to the gentle, open-ended questions, such as, "Hey, are you doing okay?" and "You want to talk?" This lets your child know you are there for her, you're interested in her well-being, and what she's going through.

It's not uncommon for older children to look to their friends for support. They may feel that they can express things to them that might not be well received by you. Don't take offense. Be glad that at least your child is talking to someone, rather than going into a state of withdrawal. One of the primary purposes and functions of good friends is to be there when you need them. Give the older teenager time; there is a lot for them to consider and process.

Ironically, the younger children tend to be much more resilient. It's kind of a blessed coping gift, which provides them with a defense. Because their maturity level isn't as high, the issues they perceive are not as complex. They are still at that age where whatever Mommy and Daddy say must be right because Mommy and Daddy said it. The four year old will be more concerned as to whether she will get to keep her toys and where she will sleep. In some ways it will be a bit easier to reassure the younger child, but it still requires focus, commitment, and monitoring.

Sometimes with young children, you can actually put a positive spin on things that they will find acceptable. "Even though Mommy and Daddy aren't living together, we both still love you. You are so special that now you get to have two houses and two bedrooms." This is an important issue for a pre-adolescent.

What does seem to be universally important with children, especially the young ones, is that they will continue to see both parents. The fact that Mom and Dad, whom they love very much, aren't living together is one thing, but to have one of them out of their life altogether is a totally different and much bigger issue.

While this is discussed in greater detail in Chapter Seven, let me briefly state that this is the time that you have to assure your children that you will both continue to be there for them and that you are both going to be an active part of their lives. The one thing you do not want your child to experience at this time is a feeling of abandonment. A preliminary agreement of the parental peace accord between you and your spouse should be that you will both be allowed to have an active involvement in your children's lives.

Lastly, this process does not end with the finalization of your dissolution. Children grow and change, circumstances change, and new issues will develop. It is important for both parents to keep an open line of communication with their children regarding what they are feeling and how they are handling things. Just as spousal communication is the principle vehicle for success of *The Parental Peace Accord*, communication between parents and their children is just as vital. Age is not a factor here. The communication is just as important whether we're discussing a T-ball game or helping our child make wedding plans.

Notes and Thoughts

_____

_____

_____

_____

_____

_____

_____

_____

_____

_____

_____

_____

_____

_____

_____

_____

_____

_____

_____

_____

_____

_____

_____

_____

_____

_____

4 | SEAL THY LIPS

When two parents are working to have a parental peace accord, more important than knowing what to say to your children is knowing what *not* to say. Oh, how easy it would be to tell our children of how we were wronged by our ex-spouses. And it certainly seems appropriate for our children to know that Dad is a womanizer or Mom is a compulsive psycho freak. After all, we want our children to be able to recognize these behaviors so they may steer clear of them and not marry into the same mistakes that you did. Right?

Come on now, who are you kidding? You can use any method you want to try to justify this kind of behavior, but the fact is, you're doing it for yourself and certainly not for your children. Perhaps you're doing it because you feel you need to justify the divorce to your child. Maybe it's your way of getting back at your spouse or ex because of the hurt you have felt. Or it might be that you're just a mean-hearted person who doesn't realize the verbal barbs that you're hurling could be hurting the ones you love the most, your children.

Bad-mouthing

There is an old saying: It's nice to be smart, but it's smart to be nice. Unfortunately, many parents forget this in the heat of the divorce battlefield or in the life afterwards. Emotions and stress run high, and it's pretty easy to start casting stones toward, our adversaries. We hurt; therefore they should hurt. And we know just what to say or do to inflict the appropriate amount of pain. So it seems only natural that there would be a few things our children should know about their other parent. Why, it's the responsible thing to do!

Maybe, but I doubt it. Certainly there are situations that may have to be addressed. Abuse, murder, neglect and abandonment are examples, just to name a few. However, the manner in which these issues are addressed with our children is critical. It is one thing to label the other parent, while it is an entirely different thing to address the conduct of the other parent. There is a big difference between saying, "Your father is a no good, rotten so-and-so," as opposed to saying, "What your father did was very wrong," or "I was very hurt by your father's conduct."

Okay, why is this so important? Am I splitting hairs? Remember my experiences as a child in the orphanage in Orange County that I discussed in the last chapter. I lived with a number of kids who had been physically and emotionally abused by their parents. These kids had the scars to prove it. Many of them were afraid of their parents and knew that they had been mistreated. But amazingly enough, they still loved those parents and wanted to be with them, even though it wasn't in their best interest! Of course there were some that were filled with anger and hate, but the majority still loved their parents and would have left the orphanage in a minute to be with them.

To bad-mouth your spouse or ex-spouse is a no-win situation. Contrary to what you may think, you are not going to score any points with your child, and in fact, you run the risk of losing the "game" entirely. I have heard so many horror stories regarding the statements parents have said about each other to their children. Imagine this dialogue between a young teenage girl and her father during a visitation:

Daughter: "Mom dyed her hair."

Father: "Yeah, I saw her. She looks like a whore."

Now what this idiot father didn't know was that his daughter liked her Mom's new look and didn't feel that just because Mom died her hair blonde that it made her look like a whore. So what was the father's point? Did he think making such a statement would win his daughter over to his side? Did making such a statement to his daughter make him feel better because he got to vent some anger stemming from the dissolution? Did he think the daughter was going to say, "Gee, Dad, I'm so glad you said that because I feel exactly the same way?"

No, the fact is he didn't think at all. The first thing he forgot was that the statement wasn't being made to just *his* daughter. More importantly, and never to be forgotten, he was also saying it to *Mom's* daughter. Think about how most people would feel if someone made such a statement about their mother. The response would probably be anger at best, a bloody nose at worst.

Women can be just as stupid and insensitive as men. I can't count the number of times I've heard of mothers asking their children things like, "So who's that slut your Dad is hanging around with?" Smart, real smart. You're talking about your child's father. Even if the new woman in your ex's life does not live up to your standards, this is not a judgment call you should make in front of his children. If you love them, let them come to their own conclusions.

Okay, I've been pretty hard on the people who are making these mistakes. Are they really stupid, and are they really idiots? Probably not. They are probably so wrapped up in their own emotional turmoil that they don't realize the damage they can cause with such caustic statements or observations. But in doing so, they've forgotten the principle foundation of a successful parental peace accord. It's about the child, not you.

To have the greatest positive impact on your child, you should not only refrain from bad-mouthing the other parent, but you should try to be supportive of the other parent. If your ex has decided to go back to school, tell your child what a good thing that is and how they should be proud of Mom or Dad. There's something to be said for always taking "the high road." It gives a positive message to your children and makes you look good in their eyes. If the things you say come from the gutter, you're just going to always seem dirty to your children.

I knew of a couple that had gotten divorced. Dad built a very nice, expensive, custom-built home. Mom, who had more limited resources, purchased a very nice middle-class home in a stable neighborhood.

Dad went on to tell their daughters that the houses in their Mom's neighborhood weren't safe and that they were very susceptible to fires—all of which was unfounded and untrue.

All that Dad's one-upmanship did was to instill fear in his daughters that their house might burn down. The girls didn't think, "Oh, Dad's house is so much better than Mom's." Instead they thought, "Oh my, what if the house catches on fire while I'm asleep?" It's hard to believe that the unbridled emotions of divorced parents can cause them to unintentionally create such pain and havoc in their children's lives.

How hard is it, out of love for your children, to take the opposite approach and be positive? You apparently loved your ex at one point in time and felt he or she was a good enough partner with whom to bring children into the world. So why is it so difficult to be supportive of our children and to tell them how they are lucky to have two parents who love them so much? Why is it so hard to acknowledge the accomplishments of our ex-spouses for the benefit of our children? And why do parents refuse to communicate with each other when their children's lives and happiness may be dependent upon it?

There are hundreds of books that address the topic of a positive mental attitude. It has been proven to be effective in business, self-esteem, personal relationships, as well as first and last impressions. I would submit to you that the same holds true for the dynamics of a divorced family. If your children hear positive things come out of their parents' mouths, and they observe a positive attitude, they in turn will have a positive outlook on the things around them, including their family's situation.

I've said it before, and I will continue to say it: Every child is entitled to feel loved and have a happy childhood. This doesn't take money. We've all bought expensive presents for our toddlers only to see them have a lot more fun playing in the boxes they came in. The ingredients for a happy childhood are a positive environment, a generous helping of love, and a sprinkling of fun. Just because you are going through a divorce, or just came out of one, doesn't mean your child can't have a happy childhood.

This can only happen through a positive environment. And a positive environment can't exist if the parents are continually bad-mouthing each other, whether privately, or worse, in the presence of their children. If you find yourself doing this, stop it! There is nothing to be gained from it and everything to lose. You may have a momentary good feeling after firing a nice verbal jab at your ex in front of your children, but that feeling is like a vicious drug, one that will consume you and destroy you and your children. Your children deserve better than that.

A Child Will Figure Things Out

"But Bailey, you don't understand. Their father really is a monster, and all those things I said about him to the children are true. Don't they deserve to know the truth?" I've heard it before. My response is quite simple: Don't underestimate your children. Usually, whatever is true, they will figure out for themselves in due time.

If your ex-spouse is the monster that you claim, and you are setting a good example, your children will recognize the downfalls of the other parent. In fact, over time your children will recognize character flaws in *both* of you. It's the teenage way. And when they do acknowledge that one of their parents is something less than he or she should be, they will deal with it in their own way.

The fact that children are able to recognize right and wrong over time is the good news, and the bad news. The parent who has put the focus on their child before themselves will be rewarded with a long, lasting relationship with that child. The parents who only thinks of themselves and who put their children in the backseats of their lives will be distanced from them, or worse, have no relationship with them at all.

Through my law practice, I know a very dear woman who had the unfortunate experience of being married to an alcoholic. They had three beautiful daughters. As the alcoholism took over the man's life, a divorce became inevitable. Of course you know the rest of the story. As a result of the divorce, he drank more and more until the liquid

36

addiction became more important to him than anything else in the world, including his beautiful daughters.

As hard as I'm sure it was, when her daughters were around, this woman never spoke ill of their father. When he came up in the conversation, if there was an opportunity for bad-mouthing, the mother would refrain, saying, "It is so sad that your father's life has taken such a terrible turn. I know that deep in his heart he loves you." These are certainly not the kind of comments one would expect from an alcoholic's ex-spouse.

As time went on, the girls saw their father less and less. It seemed they always had something else they needed to do. In time, when they became older, they quit seeing their father altogether. It was a decision they made on their own, one without any undue influence from their mother. The father had never sent any Christmas or birthday cards, much less gifts. He didn't acknowledge weddings. There was truly no relationship between the daughters and their father.

Their mother went on to marry again. Her new husband was a police officer and a wonderful man. He grew to love those girls. The alcoholism eventually claimed the life of their biological father. Their mother attended the funeral services; however, the daughters refused, saying he had never been a father to them, and it would be hypocritical for them to attend the funeral of a man they didn't know and who had never acknowledged their existence. "Besides," they said, "we have a father," referring to their stepfather.

Here's the part you need to understand. The respect and high esteem these girls (young women now, with children of their own) have for their mother is what every parent would want from their children. As the daughters became older, they realized what it must have been like for their mother, living with an alcoholic, raising three daughters on her own, and trying to make ends meet. And yet, they never heard her complain. They never heard her bad-mouth their father for the plight he had created. Her behavior made them realize what a special and honorable person their mother is. The relationship between this mother and her daughters is as close as it could be and now her children will be there for *her* for the rest of her life.

I have one last point to make with this story, and then I'll move on. If you were to ask this woman about her children's father today, years and years after his death, she would simply say, "It's unfortunate; he had such a tragic life." You see, putting her children first and saying what was best became natural for her. Imagine how different the dynamics of this story would have been if she had spent her daughters' childhoods ranting and raving about what a drunken SOB their father was and how he didn't deserve to live.

Part of putting our children first is taking the high road, even when we don't really want to take that route. But as the Nike slogan goes, "Just do it." It will certainly be a lot less stressful. Think about it. When you bad-mouth, all you are doing is engaging in negative emotions, which in turn, create stress. If you let it go with a noncommittal positive comment, it's over and you can move on. Make it a game if you have to. Ask yourself, "How can I avoid making a negative comment in this part of the discussion?"

Here are some examples. Your child comes home from visiting with his mother and says, "I'm telling you, I think that woman is psycho!" Well there are two things you can say. You can say, "You don't have to tell me; why do you think I divorced her?" Or you can say, "Well, she's probably feeling a lot of stress right now, just try to be tolerant." Now seriously, which response do you think is the more positive of the two and which one puts you in a more favorable light to your child? You might think that siding with your child will be a bonding thing, but that is a very dangerous way to think. The feelings your child expresses in anger or frustration may not be his true feelings. If you buy into those negative statements, he will remember what you said long after his anger or frustration has disappeared.

Here's another example. Your children say, "Dad is so compulsive! It's like it's a major crisis if everything isn't in its place and just so. He makes me crazy." Well, Mom could say, "Oh I know, everything has to be done your Dad's way or all hell will break loose." Or if she's really thinking about the long-term effects on her children, she might say, "I think its probably just his way of wanting to have a nice home for you, one that you can be proud of. Everybody has different priorities." In the latter case, Mom hasn't jumped on the bandwagon; instead she has diffused the situation without dismissing her child's feelings.

Here's my last example, which is a true story. A father commits the ultimate sin by not showing up to pick up his five year-old daughter for visitation, and to make matters worse, doesn't even call. The daughter, whose name is Kelly (not really), is heartbroken, as she was looking forward to spending time with Daddy. She feels a bit unloved at the moment. Her terrific mother, her name is Julie (false again), could have expressed her frustration by raving about what an insensitive, irresponsible moron Kelly has for a father. Instead, she sits on the couch with her daughter, wraps her in her arms, and says, "I'm sure something came up that kept Daddy from being here, but you know what? You're my most favoritest Kelly in the whole wide world, and Mommies never stop loving their Kellys!" That response is always met with a giggle that would melt any parent's heart.

Again, as children grow older they will come to their own conclusions about their parents. This is true whether their parents are divorced or not. Your children will be better served if you let them reach those conclusions on their own without help or manipulation from you. Most importantly, your child will hold you in greater esteem for taking the high road. You have more control over this than you think.

When you really feel the urge to rip your ex in front of your children, take a lesson I've used in raising my sons. I've told them that everything in life is about choices and consequences. Every choice they make will have a positive or negative consequence. If they make a choice that could have a negative consequence, they must decide whether it was worth it.

For instance, if they make the choice to study, a natural consequence might be better grades. On the other hand, if they make the choice to watch MTV instead of studying, they have to decide if watching that particular show was worth the consequence of coming home with a poor grade.

I've always told them the same rule applies for adults. Every morning when I wake up I have an immediate choice to make. I can stay in bed and doze off into a deep slumber or I can get up, shower, shave, get dressed, and go to work. Although on some mornings I might prefer to stay in bed, I'm just not willing to pay the consequences of that decision. I'll get behind, and as a result, disappoint people, set a bad example, and feel guilty—all of which will create stress. So I choose to get my butt out of bed, because the other choice is just not worth the resulting consequences.

On occasions when I have had to punish or reprimand my children, choices and consequences are always part of the discussion. I might say, "Son, you made this choice and it wasn't a good choice. And because it wasn't a good choice it has negative consequences, one of which has to be some form of punishment." (Trust me, this approach really takes the anger out of the equation and sends the message that the punishment is out of love.)

So, you might consider doing a little self-analysis of the choices you make and their potential consequences the next time you feel the urge to bad-mouth your child's mom or dad. Engage your brain before your mouth. Ask yourself, "If I make this response, is it really putting my child first, what will the long term effects be, and how does it make me look to my child?"

As I have said before, bad-mouthing is a losing strategy at best. It puts you in a negative light in your child's eyes. It puts you in a negative and stressful frame of mind. It has the very real potential of backfiring on you. And last, but not least, you run the risk of your ex retaliating with his own bad-mouthing, which could escalate into a childish game of "who can have the last word."

Take the high road. Put your child's best interest before the expression of your own emotions. And above all, give your children some credit for eventually figuring things out for themselves about you and your ex. Children aren't stupid. There are a lot of parents who think their children don't see or recognize things going on around them. Don't kid yourself. They get it. And even when you think they're not listening, they are.

So you're in control. The choice is yours. You can take the high road or the low road, positive or negative. It's about your kids. Don't blow it.

Notes and Thoughts

_____

_____

_____

_____

_____

_____

_____

_____

_____

_____

_____

_____

_____

_____

_____

_____

_____

_____

_____

5 | Negotiations

Here is something you should know. From this point forward and until your children reach adulthood, the entirety of the relationship between you and your ex-spouse will consist of a series of negotiations. Although you may not believe this, you have the option to decide whether this is going to be a tolerable, low-stress activity, or a nightmare from hell. From this point forward, you and your ex-spouse can either be in control of the decisions affecting your child's welfare, or you can let some stranger in a black robe, someone who doesn't know your child from any other, make the decisions for you.

Now this seems like a no-brainer, right? I mean, what parent in their right mind would want some Judge No-Name deciding what is best for a child he or she doesn't know? The judge doesn't know your child loves gymnastics. The judge doesn't know your child is an honor student. The judge doesn't know your child's favorite vacation spot is Gulf Shores, Alabama. *The judge doesn't know your child!*

So why would you and your child's other parent want this person, who knows nothing about your child, to decide what is best for your child? The fact is that the majority of parents can't get beyond their own emotional turmoil, which unintentionally puts their children's best interest on the back burner. Parents don't mean to do it; it's just that everything gets real cloudy.

I know a lot of judges, and I have sat on the bench myself in a *pro tempore* capacity. I can assure you that almost every judge I know would rather see the parents come to an agreement in dissolution and post-dissolution proceedings. This is not because they want to get out of work. It is because they understand that in most cases the parents are in the best position to decide what is best for their children, and if they can agree, it is a sign that these two parents have the capacity to work together in determining the future of their child.

Pick Your Battles

Conversely, there are some parents who don't have a clue and will never be able to work together. I have seen divorce clients argue over a five-dollar Gillette razor. I have seen them spend eight hundred dollars in attorney fees arguing over a seventy-five-dollar lawn mower. And if you think the attorneys enjoy earning their hourly rate arguing over safety razors and lawn mowers, you couldn't be more wrong. They have their tolerance levels too. And yet, it will be those same clients, who argued over razors and lawn mowers, who will scream to the high heavens when they get the bills from their respective attorneys. Sometimes it just doesn't make sense.

When it comes to negotiations, rule number one is to pick your battles. What is really important in the grand scheme of things? Are the things you find yourself arguing about really worth the stress, attorney's fees, delays, and aggravation? Probably not. But if you want to pay for people to argue about these things on your behalf, there are always attorneys who will do just that. But if you and your spouse or ex-spouse have chosen this route, I have some bad news for you. Nobody wins.

Even if you think you won, you probably didn't. I represented a multi-millionaire in a divorce who had only been married a few months. Nevertheless, the bride wanted half of his wealth; even though the marriage was only months old and she had brought nothing into the marital estate. You guessed it. We went to trial, and the judge decided she was only entitled to a little over sixty thousand dollars. Here's the best part. My multi-millionaire client was furious with the judgment because in his emotional opinion, she wasn't entitled to a thing! Oh, but it gets even better. He decided he was going to appeal the decision.

Enough is enough. I told him that although he certainly had the right to appeal the ruling, he needed to find other counsel. Nobody wins.

Adults Only, No Children Allowed

If there is one thing a child should not be involved in, it is negotiations between his parents. And if there is one place he shouldn't be, it is at the negotiation table. It doesn't matter if that negotiation table is located in your attorney's office or in your kitchen, your children don't belong there.

Parents do their children a great disservice when they try to bring them into the haggling of property distribution, custody, child support, and visitation. Your child is going through enough turmoil as it is because his mother and father are splitting up; he doesn't need to be put in the middle of a "who is going to get the washer and dryer" argument. This may seem obvious to you, but oh, to walk a mile in my shoes.

The real secret to making this area a part of your parental peace accord is to agree to discuss every decision on the basis of what is best for the children. This approach really does put the focus where it needs to be, and, if done sincerely, it has a way of taking the personality of the parents out of the equation.

As I mentioned in the first chapter of this book, once my ex-wife and I came to an agreement to base our decisions on what was best for the children, it resolved about 90 percent of the issues we could have been arguing about. Oh, we had a lot of "stuff" to divide up: a nice home, nice cars, residential rental property, commercial rental property, a law practice, and other businesses. But when you put all of that in the perspective of "what will work out best for the kids," the answers seem to come a lot easier. So easy, in fact, that all of those decisions were eventually made by us, not a judge. When we put our agreement in writing for the judge to sign, we knew we had made the best decisions for our children. (And yes, my wife did have her own attorney.)

If you are committed to having a parental peace accord with your spouse or ex-spouse, you have to be willing to set aside your emotions so that, you can see the forest and not just the trees. The best place to start is with property. Yes, I know you worked hard for it and you're entitled to this or that, but the fact is that it is just "stuff." Whether it is a beautiful home, a large business, or your favorite collection, in the eyes of the court it is just "stuff" to be divided.

This is not to say your tangible property doesn't have value. To the contrary, if the two of you can't agree on values and division, placing a value on your property is exactly what the court will do. If the two of you can't agree on what that Newbury dining room set is worth, you can hire an appraiser for a few hundred bucks an hour, your spouse can hire an appraiser for a few hundred bucks an hour, and for a unbiased, third opinion, the court can appoint an appraiser for a few hundred bucks an hour. And hey, if all those appraisers can't agree, hell, we'll just add up their appraisals, divide it by three, and come up with a nice average value for that dining room set. In fact, we can use that same process for every stick of furniture in the house, jewelry, or anything else the two of you own. And don't worry about how much these appraisers and attorneys are charging; it will all be paid for out of the marital estate the two of you are fighting over.

Okay, I've slipped into a little bit of sarcasm again. It is very reasonable to assume that both of you are not going to have a good idea of the value of everything in your marital estate. Using reputable, certified appraisers will help you and your spouse make informed decisions. And yes, using certified appraisers is still a lot less expensive than paying attorneys for a courtroom battle. And lastly, the two of you can't be expected to know the laws of the specific jurisdiction in which you live. A good, well-recommended family law attorney can provide you with sound advice and counsel on the approach the courts in your jurisdiction take toward dissolution and post-dissolution issues.

The question is, are you going to let these professionals provide you and your parenting partner with information so the two of you can make informed decisions as to what will be best for your children, or are you going to fight each other and pay these professionals to argue or make the decision for you? Will it be best for the children, based on finances, for Mom or Dad to have the house? Is Mom or Dad more qualified to run the family business so that it can provide a source of college funds for the children? Will taking the furniture out of the house have a negative impact on the children's sense of stability and security?

If you can't look at these property issues from an unemotional standpoint, believe me, the court can. Your attorney can tell you the statutory provisions for division of marital estates in your specific jurisdiction. Generally speaking, most jurisdictions start at an equal division of marital property, then allow for certain considerations that may or may not move the needle from the fifty-percent mark. Talk to your attorney and find out what the standard is in your jurisdiction. And quit listening to everybody else regarding what happened in *their* divorce. It has nothing to do with yours, and it certainly has nothing to do with your children.

Now, we talked earlier about how children don't belong in the negotiations or even at the negotiating table. This does not mean they don't have anything to do with the negotiations. They have everything to do with the negotiations, just not active participation. The whole point is that you are deciding issues on what is best for the children on a long-term basis. There are no set rules for this because all children have different personalities, needs, and interests.

So you probably think I'm talking out of both sides of my mouth. Not really. This is another situation where parents have to walk a fine line. You want your child's input, but you don't want to ask them for it. So you have to engage in that parent thing of knowing your children better than anybody else—especially that guy in the black robe.

How old are your children? What makes them happy? What is going to make them feel secure and cause the least disruption in their lives? Which parent do they identify with? (Suck it up and be honest.) What is going to make it easy for both Mom and Dad to continue to be active participants in their lives? What sends the message to them that Mom and Dad are still united as parents, even if not by marriage?

These are the things the two of you have to figure out. Is it difficult? Yes. Yes, because it will require the two of you to set your marital differences aside and engage in some very intense, meaningful communication. Is it impossible? No. No, because the two of you are in the best position to know what is best for your children, and there has never been a better or more appropriate circumstance to use the "two heads are better than one" approach. I know these discussions take an enormous emotional stretch. I know most people will tell you that you're living in la-la land to even think it can work. But it can, and it has.

There are divorced parents all around you who have resolved their divorces through a settlement agreement and who maintain a civil, and oftentimes warm, relationship with each other. They do it out of a life-long common bond, one which is based upon the love they share for their children. The problem is, you don't hear about them. Instead you hear about the husband who found all of his personal belongings in the front yard. You hear about the couple who liquidated everything they had, fighting until the bitter end, only to tell everybody "those damn lawyers got it all." You hear about the woman who can't buy her kids school clothes because her ex-husband isn't paying child support. This is what people talk about, and this is what you hear. Meanwhile there are divorced parents all around you shaking their heads in disbelief at these stories. People don't talk much about them; it's just not as exciting.

So why can't you just ask the kids? Although you may want their input, you don't want them to feel like they are in the middle. I'm reminded of a mother in the middle of a divorce who brought her thirteen-year-old son in the living room and told his father, "Look your son in the eye and tell him what you think I should have out of this damn marriage." Obviously, this is not a good tactic at all. It is clear the Mom's emotions got in the way of good common sense. Dragging her child into the living room and putting him in the middle of the discussion was not what was best for her son.

As strange as it may seem, the biggest challenge many parents have in figuring out what is important to their children is just *listening*. Parents get so involved in mentoring their children, telling them what is right from wrong and giving their unsolicited opinion, they forget to just shut up and listen. If you just let your children do the talking, they will give you a lot of insight as to what is important in their lives.

Lastly, there is another reason you shouldn't just ask your child what is best for them. They often don't know. Certainly, this would come as no surprise if we are dealing with a toddler or adolescent. But the fact is that a lot of older teenagers don't really have a handle on what is best for them. They don't have your experience. They don't have your common sense (in most cases). And in some cases, you know them better than they know themselves. That's why you're the parent and have all the responsibility.

Money

If it isn't obvious, you should know that children have no business in negotiations regarding money. First of all, the previous reasons we've discussed, such as being placed in the middle, all apply. But more importantly, kids really don't have a good concept of money. This is true whether we are talking about a five year old or an eighteen year old.

A mother recently told me about a three-day trip she went on with her daughters to Nashville, Tennessee. They stayed at the Gaylord Opryland Resort in a room overlooking the beautiful nine-acre garden atrium. The room cost them a little over $250 per night. Her seven-year-old daughter said she thought it would be really cool to stay in the suite. The mother said that would be nice, but she thought the suite ran about $3,500 per night. "That's okay," the little girl replied, "we could just stay for one night."

The concept of money doesn't get much better with teenagers. In an effort to teach our son the value of money, my ex-wife and I told him that when he was ready to buy a car, we would split it three ways between him, his mother, and me. In other words, when the time came, for every dollar he had to put toward a car, together his mother and I would match it with two dollars. He came home pretty excited one day because he had just bought a new Dave Matthews CD for about thirteen dollars. I told him it must be a great CD for him to spend thirty-nine dollars. He gave me a puzzled look and asked me what I meant. I informed him that it was thirteen dollars he wouldn't have to put toward his car and that sounded like thirty-nine dollars to me. You could just see the wheels turning in his head as the concept sunk in.

Regardless of their age, your children will not have a good concept of money. They don't have the financial responsibilities that we have as adults. They don't work forty or more hours a week, then come home and spend all their earnings on exciting stuff like electricity, food, and mortgage payments. And they shouldn't, they're kids. But it is kind of amusing to watch them get that first paycheck from their part-time job. They figured their hours and hourly rate, and they finally get their first check. They see something wrong with the check. Their boss shorted them about 35 percent. That's when you have to explain taxes to them, and they get their first dose of financial reality.

So leave the children out of the monetary negotiations because they really don't have a clue. It doesn't matter whether you and you parenting partner are discussing property settlement, the amount of child support, or college education funds; the two of you should be able to figure out what is best for your child without his or her involvement. You've both had a lot more experience at it than him or her.

I have one last point on this matter. If you and your spouse were to continue to be married, in all likelihood, your children would not be subjected to discussions regarding child support or property divisions. So why should this burdensome topic be placed on their shoulders now? They deserve the same carefree childhood they would have had if Mom and Dad had worked things out.

I can honestly say that in the last fourteen years, my children have never asked me about the child support arrangements between their mother and me. This is probably because the child support arrangements were just that, between their mother and me. Certainly, my oldest son knows I am paying for his college education because the bursar sends him the bills, and I pay them. But I think I can safely say that neither of my sons have ever heard their mother and I discuss monetary matters in front of them; it's just an unwritten rule of *our* parental peace accord.

This is in contrast to the parents who tell their children to ask their other parent when they can expect to get the child support payment. All that does is reduce your child to a messenger and sends the negative message that the other parent is not responsible. This is not a task that contributes to your children having a happy, carefree childhood. This should be an adults-only conversation between you and your parenting partner. Pick up the phone, fire off an e-mail, or leave a voice mail. And be nice.

Hopefully, what I have discussed in this chapter will be not be misinterpreted as a directive to parents not to educate their children on money matters and financial responsibility. That's a different issue. With all the games that credit card companies and banks are playing these days, your children need all the advice and counsel you can give them. Unfortunately, the schools aren't doing a great job of giving our kids practical lessons on money. They're doing better, but there is a lot of room for improvement.

What this chapter refers to are those sensitive monetary matters and negotiations that exist as a result of parents dissolving their marriage. When engaged in this, follow the premise of *The Parental Peace Accord*. It's about the children, not you. If you do this, especially in negotiations, you'll see things starting to get a lot smoother and a lot less stressful. And if the two of you do a really good job, you just might not have to pay your attorneys quite as much!

Notes and Thoughts

6 | A Brief Look At Custody

First of all, I have to tell you that, in my opinion, the title of this chapter is contradictory. Custody is a very complex area, and there is nothing brief about its consideration. Because no two custody situations are the same, I am forced to discuss generalities, which will lend to a certain amount of brevity. In most divorce cases involving children, custody is the most sensitive issue for everybody: Mom, Dad, the children, and the judge. There is just no way around it. The lives of the children are going to be changed as to their living arrangements, whether they're living with Dad, Mom, or equally with both. Your approach to this issue is critical and has a direct relationship to the degree of difficulty your children will experience.

It's About The Kids, Not You

Let's begin with the foundation of *The Parental Peace Accord*. It's about the children, not you. Very few parents want to lose the pleasure they have in living with their children. In fact, it is probably the worst nightmare of parents, second only to the death of a child. Such devastation evokes visions of missing the development and life experiences of our children, broken holidays, lost quiet moments, and dysfunctional relationships. With all of these fears going on, it is damn near impossible to set aside our emotions so that we can be objective about what is best for our children. Impossible or not, it must be done. Nobody said raising children was going to be easy, and this is one of those times when each of us must suck it up and be a caring, loving, responsible parent, even if it is mental torture. Our children deserve it.

You have to ask yourself a hard question: "What custody arrangement will be best for my child and disrupt her life the least?" More importantly, you have to answer that question with blunt, painful honesty. You know the answer. You just may not be willing to come to grips with it. Now is the time to tell yourself the truth, no matter how painful it may be. It requires courage, but your child's happiness and well-being depend on it.

I'm reminded of the mother who screamed, "I will never let anyone take away my children!" It didn't matter to her that she had three drunk-driving convictions, had dropped out of Alcohol Anonymous twice, and hadn't had a sober week in three years. What mattered to her was that she couldn't imagine her life without her children. To her, not having her children was the last straw in a life that had gone terribly out of control. She felt that losing her children would be losing any chance of overcoming her addiction.

The problem is that every one of her thoughts and concerns was about herself. What about the children? Where did they fit into her selfish thoughts and concerns? Was it really going to be in the best interest of the children she loved so much to come home from school every day to find Mom laying on the sofa passed out? Was it in the children's best interest to be placed in harm's way the first time Mom drove them somewhere drunk and without a license? Of course not, and a case with this type of extreme example is usually fairly easy for a judge to sort out.

Unfortunately, the situations and determinations are not always so obvious. There are so many factors that can play into what will be best for the child. The parents and the courts must consider the child's age, interests, physical and emotional needs, relationships with Mom and Dad, as well as the lifestyle and employment requirements of the parents. Consider the different needs of a two year old compared to those of a teenager who is getting his driver's license. Compare the son who is following in Dad's all-star-sports footsteps to the daughter who shares a love of dance with her Mom. Look at the availability of a parent who has employment responsibilities that require traveling all through the week as compared to a parent who works locally and is home every night. Now mix all of these variables plus hundreds more together, and you begin to see why custody has to be determined on a case-by-case basis.

It's About The Kids, Not Child Support

Here's a consideration that never ceases to amaze me. I can't tell you how many times I have found parents considering child support as a custody issue. "If she gets the kids, the child support will kill me!" Suffice it to say the priorities are a little out of whack with these people. Child support should not be a determining factor or a bartering tool in child custody. It is a completely different issue with a completely different set of considerations.

In most jurisdictions, the objective of the court regarding child support is to allow the children to continue living at or close to the standard of living they would have enjoyed had the divorce not occurred. While this objective sounds good in principle, it can certainly prove unrealistic at times. However, the objective of the court regarding custody is to determine what is in the best interest of the child. The support issue is nothing more than a function of mathematics, while the custody issue embraces the mental and emotional future of the child. Obviously, these are two very separate issues. Accordingly, if you are considering child support as a determinant for deciding which custody arrangement is best for your children, you are very misguided.

Child support is an issue to be decided *after* custody. Additionally, in most jurisdictions, child support can take a lot of different forms. It is more than a periodic payment that you would budget for along with your mortgage and car payments. It may take the form of medical bills, college expenses, and extracurricular activities. In some jurisdictions the judge will determine this unilaterally, while other jurisdictions have very complex tables and formulas used to calculate the support responsibilities of each parent.

The first blush reaction to parents who consider child support a determining factor for custody is that they want awarded custody so they don't have to pay child support. I have found some parents to think just the opposite. These ill-advised fools think that if the other parent has custody, they will be the ones on the hook for medical and dental bills, as well as sports and extracurricular expenses. If the custodial parent isn't paid, he or she is the one who is in danger of having his or her credit wrecked. In fact, some non-custodial parents have been known to put off paying their portion of a bill just to create havoc in the lives of their ex-spouses. It is clear that parents who engage in this conduct and way of thinking are being irresponsible toward their children's needs, and in many cases, still harbor feelings of resentment for their ex-spouses as a result of the divorce. They obviously don't get it. It's about the children, not them.

It's About The Kids, Not What People Think

Another common issue that arises regarding custody is the fear of what people will think of the parent who is not awarded custody. There are so many divorcees who can't bear to face people at work, church, and social circles. They feel that they are now stigmatized, and everybody will be talking about them behind their backs. They feel their friends will think they have to take a side and pledge their continued friendship to one or the other. Well, there is something to this, even though it is not nearly as much of a factor as it was during our parents' generation. The sad truth is that divorce has become so common that most people don't discuss it anymore after initial awareness.

However, the parents who have concerns about what people will think with respect to their divorce are even more concerned about what people will think if they don't have custody of their children. Unfortunately, this emotion seems to present itself more often in mothers than fathers. The reason is pretty simple. It is a throwback to the traditional thinking that a man provides for the family and that a woman's place is in the home. While our society has made great strides in moving past this and recognizing that these roles are not gender determined, there is still a residual concern among many women that people will have a "What kind of mother is she?" reaction to a father having custody. And I regret to report that there are still some judges on the bench who also haven't moved beyond traditional gender-role thinking.

The good news is that most of society and judges are getting away from this. They realize that a father can change diapers and feed the baby just as proficiently as a mother can go out and have a financially successful career. They recognize that the ability to hold down a job or to raise children is not based on gender. The old assumption by parents that a judge will automatically grant custody to the mother is often mistaken. I have had many father-clients who received custody of their children. It's about the children, not gender.

It's A Home, Not A House

It's about the custody arrangement that will provide the children with the most stable environment and the least amount of disruption in their lives. Try to take your emotions out of the equation. You know your children. What is going to provide them with a stable home? Not a house, a home. What will give them a home where they can feel warmth, security, and happiness? If you take the approach these questions suggest, you are on the right track. Fortunately, because most parents know what is best for their children, the majority of divorce cases with children reach an agreement on custody issues. Again, you know your children and their needs far better than some stranger in a black robe. You and your spouse have a choice.

As parents who care about and know their children, you can determine what is best for them. Or as parents who are trapped on the emotional roller coaster of self-interest, outward appearances, and financial leverage, you can let a judge who knows nothing about your children make the decisions for you. This latter path will be unpleasant and expensive for you. More tragically, it will take an unfortunate situation and make it a living nightmare for the children you love so much. If custody becomes a contested issue, there are no winners.

Parents are stressed, their characters are attacked, children are torn, courts are clogged, and attorney fees are high. If child custody is going to be a disputed issue, strap yourself in; it's going to be a rough and rocky ride for everybody involved.

Disputed Custody, An Ugly Place To Be

You see, in most jurisdictions, especially those with no-fault "irretrievable breakdown of the marriage" statutes, a good share of dissolution issues are resolved by the numbers. Property division statutes may dictate a fifty-fifty split, and the presumptive positioning of the needle may be adjusted by certain circumstances. Child support may be calculated by a formula or table adopted by the court. Even the responsibility for attorney fees may be dictated by the income of the parties. Hire a good, well-recommended family law attorney, and he or she can fill you in on the approach your specific jurisdiction utilizes.

Custody, however, is a completely different animal. Most jurisdictions use a "best interest of the child" standard to determine which parent should be awarded custody. Obviously, if the issue is contested, the parents become adversaries. In other words, each parent is forced to present evidence to the court as to why it is in the child's best interest to be in his or her custody. Unfortunately, that needed evidence often comes in the form of attacking the other parent's character to show why it is *not* in the child's best interest to be with them. This scenario often gets extremely ugly.

This is where all the dirty laundry gets aired. Mom is putting in evidence to show that Dad is an irresponsible womanizer who can't be trusted. Dad is putting in evidence to show that Mom is mentally unstable. Dad is a drunk! Mom is a whore! Oh, and by the way, here are some of our friends who will testify to the truthfulness of our allegations. Little, insignificant occurrences become glaring evidence of why we are not fit to have custody of our child. I assume you're starting to get the picture here, but it gets worse. Guess who inadvertently gets to experience the pain and turmoil of this emotional disaster? You guessed it—the children!

My sons and I are huge movie buffs. We play a private, fun game in which we carry on an entire conversation using lines from various movies. Okay, maybe it's one of those bonding things. When it comes to contested custody issues, one of the best movies I have ever seen is *Kramer vs. Kramer* starring Dustin Hoffman and Meryl Streep. I didn't say it was a happy movie. On the contrary, it paints a very realistic and painful picture of how contested custody can escalate and become out of control. Anyone who doesn't feel like working with the other parent to come to an agreement on custody should watch this film.

Unfortunately, in the game of contested custody, the stakes keep getting higher. It is absolutely shocking to witness the levels parents will sink to in an effort to gain custody of their children. This behavior usually stems from emotional hurt and turmoil, which makes it about winning the war, not the children. I'll give you an example from one of the ugliest cases I have ever been involved in and one which showed the greatest abuse and frailties of the system.

The System Can Fail

I represented a father whose wife had fallen in love and run off with another man. Not only did she want to live happily ever after with her new found love, she didn't want her soon-to-be ex to be in any part of her life or in any part of their four-year-old daughter's life. They had been separated for months, with the mother having temporary custody and the father having temporary alternating weekend visitation. Things were extremely tense, to say the least. Then the bombshell was dropped.

The mother went to the child welfare department in the county where she lived and claimed she had reason to believe that her estranged husband was sexually abusing their daughter. As should happen in such circumstances, an extensive investigation was commenced, and the father's temporary visitation rights were suspended until further notice by the court presiding over the divorce proceedings.

The child was brought in for an interview with a welfare worker. The interview was video recorded. The child was asked if she liked her Daddy. Was her Daddy nice to her? Did she like visiting with her Daddy? Did she and her Daddy have fun together? Did she love her Daddy? The little girl responded affirmatively to all of these questions; it was obvious she was quite fond of her Daddy and that he was a special person in her life.

The welfare worker then asked the little girl if her Daddy ever committed a "bad touch." This is a term used to describe inappropriate touching when communicating with small children. The daughter replied, "No." She was then asked if her Daddy ever gave her baths at night before she went to bed. She replied that her Daddy always gave her baths before she went to bed. When giving her a bath, did Daddy use a washcloth? She replied he did. The young girl was then asked if, during the course of giving her a bath with a washcloth, Daddy ever touched her "private parts." She replied that yes, he washed her all over. The interview was just under an hour, which might not seem like an enormous amount of time to us, but to a four-year-old, that's a long time.

The father was interviewed as well as the mother. In the end, and after several months, the welfare department determined that there was no evidence to support the allegation that the father had been sexually inappropriate with his daughter. The temporary visitation rights were restored during the pendency of the dissolution. End of story, right? Wrong.

The mother then reported her allegations to the prosecutor's office in the county where she was residing. The county prosecutor felt it was necessary to initiate an investigation of its own in an effort to error on the side of caution and the child's safety. Again, an extensive interview of the child was performed inquiring as to whether any "bad touch" activity by the girl's father had occurred. Again, the father and mother were interviewed as well as the maternal grandmother. Again, the temporary visitation rights of the father were suspended. The county prosecutor came to same conclusion as the welfare department; there was no evidence to support any inappropriate conduct by the father.

Temporary visitation rights were again restored. End of story, right? Wrong.

This time the mother filed a report with the welfare department of the county in which the father lived, reasoning that this was the county in which the alleged misconduct occurred. It was also the county that had jurisdiction over the divorce proceedings. Another investigation was commenced. The court again suspended all temporary visitation rights, and with the fear of "where there's smoke there must be fire," issued a no-contact order, which prohibited the father from any telephone or written communication with his daughter.

Again the daughter was extensively interviewed, all with the same results and responses. But the video recording showed that the continual questioning of this nature was starting to take a toll on the young girl. She was nervous, unhappy, and obviously afraid that she must not be giving the right answers to these repeated questions. It was also taking an emotional toll on the father. He felt helpless being caught in a "me thinks he doth protest too much" situation, and he was very concerned about what this was doing to his daughter as well as any "mind games" the mother could be playing with the daughter. The welfare department found no evidence to support the mother's claims. And no, it is not the end of the story.

As you might suspect, the mother then filed a complaint with the prosecutor's office of the father's county of residence. After requesting an emergency hearing with the dissolution court and the prosecutor, we were told that although they agreed this was a terrible thing to put a child through, one can never be too careful in these situations, and one must always error on the side of the child's safety. Accordingly, the court reactivated the visitation suspension and re-issued the no-contact order.

The father came into my law firm with tears in his eyes and said, "She wins, I quit. I can't do this anymore, and I can't watch them do this to my daughter anymore." He said one more thing. "By the way, Mr. Bailey, if this is the way the system works to protect the children, the system sucks." That was one of the few times I hated being a lawyer.

I had watched the relationship between a father and a happy, adoring daughter be destroyed by a system which was put in place to protect her.

In the end, the father agreed to allowing the mother to have custody. The second prosecutor's investigation also revealed nothing, and no charges were filed. Just to play it safe though, the court gave the father supervised visitation rights. In other words, he was allowed to spend an hour or two with his daughter in a neutral location under the watchful eye of a welfare worker. On the day of the first supervised visitation, the father and daughter had not seen each other for almost a year. The little girl cried with joy as she gave her Daddy a tight strangling hug. After a couple of years and repeated reports by the welfare worker that the two seemed very normal and appropriate with each other, the court granted the father normal visitation rights pursuant to a visitation schedule adopted by the county.

Hopefully, this story has made you furious. Furious at the system, the mother, me, the investigations, and everything else that contributed to this ugly, damaging experience. It is important that everybody protect our children from the predators in this society that prey on the young and take away their innocence and cause sexual scarring. Just as bad are those who would use those same protection devices as tools to wage a war against another innocent individual. Fortunately, if this story were to happen today, there is no doubt in my mind that the mother would have been prosecuted. And I'm relieved to report that more and more jurisdictions are vigorously pursuing false reporting charges and sentences against those who engage in this practice.

But the real lesson is how contested custody cases can turn into an emotional hurricane, destroying everything in its path. When this happens, lives are ruined, reputations are destroyed, and children are the ones who pay the price. Certainly, if you are married to an addict, an abuser, or a spouse with some other disorder that could put the children in harm's way, you have a duty to protect your children and should do everything in your power to legally and ethically obtain custody. At the same time, you have an obligation to your children to look at them and yourselves objectively and consider what is best for them, not you.

Custody, Custody, Custody

Again, consult a reputable domestic or family law attorney to ascertain the applicable custody statutes in your jurisdiction. There are various types of custody and various labels for custody in different jurisdictions. In most jurisdictions, the parent receiving custody, which is sometimes called *physical custody*, has complete, unilateral control and responsibility in determining what is best for the child. Some jurisdictions utilize the term *joint legal custody* indicating that while one parent has physical custody, both parents have input on major issues, such as education, medical, and religious decisions. Again, jurisdictions are different, and you really need to consult competent legal counsel.

Lastly, there is this thing called *joint physical custody*. With this arrangement, both parents have equal physical custody of the children with the corresponding control and responsibilities. As you might imagine, while this sounds easy in theory, it is extremely difficult in practice. In fact, I have never known a court to *order* joint physical custody in a contested custody case, although I suppose it has probably happened somewhere. The problem is that if the parents can't agree on custody, it's pretty unlikely that they will be able to agree on all the day-to-day things involved in joint physical custody.

Of course there are two distinct and common scenarios here. One involves joint physical custody between parents who live far apart and alternate physical custody for certain months or years. The other and more common scenario involves two parents who live in close proximity to each other, sharing physical custody pursuant to certain days or weeks. Both situations require a lot of work and dedication, but certainly the latter requires a lot more contact and communication between the divorced parents.

So is it possible for two people who can no longer live together and have been unable to work things out, to get along well enough to continue raising their children together in a joint physical custody setting? Possible? Absolutely! Easy? Absolutely not! Such an arrangement really requires both parents to be at the top of their games in terms of remaining civil, objective, and cordial in their implementation of *The Parental Peace Accord* principles. Although they're not married, they have to agree to be parenting partners who will work together, support each other, communicate often, and truly care about the well-being of each other. Even if you feel sure you can pull this off with the person you divorced, there are all kinds of issues just waiting to challenge this type of arrangement.

For instance, those adorable children we love so much are just that, children. And like children, they will play both ends against the middle when given the opportunity. We can all remember when we were married how the kids might say, "Dad said it is okay with him if it is okay with you," and then go out to the garage and tell Dad, "Mom said it is okay with her if it is okay with you." Or we might hear the old both ends against the middle line, "Dad lets us do it at his house," or "Mom lets me do it at her house." Well, this childhood pastime can be played a lot easier and with higher stakes if Mom and Dad don't live in the same house. And if that's not challenging enough, wait until one of the parents introduces a "significant other" into the mix. It brings the exercise of tolerance and understanding to a whole new level because it affects both parents and children. The only defense parents will have to these challenges is open and continuous communication with each other.

With this level of communication comes a great deal of sharing. The parents must tell each other what time the practices are, where the next game is, that our daughter thinks she is in love, and that our son got an after-school detention. They must also coordinate pick-up and drop-off schedules with the tenacity of an air traffic controller. They must be constantly monitoring their children to gauge how well they are coping with both parents having physical custody. It requires total and continuous involvement by both parents. It requires total and continuous support by the parents of each other.

My ex-wife and I often remark that we talk more with joint physical custody than we ever did when we were married. I also think we would both agree that we get along a lot better as parenting partners than we ever did at the time of our divorce. That's not to say that everything in a joint custody relationship is rosy and that there aren't any bumps along the way. Just the opposite is true. But the secret is how the parents go about resolving those issues. Do they have a knock-down, drag-out fight every time an issue arises? Or are they able to get their emotions under control and address the issue with their parenting partner in a civil and rational manner?

So, is joint physical custody something you should try? Probably not. You and your ex may be one of the few couples that can pull it off, but those that can are the exception, not the norm. For those who think they can do it and then can't, it's like trying to put a square peg in a round hole, and it just makes the situation worse. If there is any doubt at all, don't try it. You and your ex have to be able to look at each other and know in your heart of hearts you can say, "Yes, I am capable of this, and I know without a doubt that my ex is capable of this. I believe in his or her commitment to make this work as much as I do my own." That's pretty strong commitment for two people who just got divorced.

Knowing this, I know I am blessed—blessed to have the person who is the mother of my children to be an intelligent person, willing to make any commitment and sacrifice for the benefit of our children; blessed to have two boys who grew up to be successful well-balanced adults; and blessed to be in a situation where our sons always knew they were loved and raised by both of their parents, even though they were no longer married.

Although joint physical custody is probably the hardest thing to do, it is the ultimate reward of a true commitment to the principles of The *Parental Peace Accord*. Don't attempt joint physical custody just to say you have accomplished the ultimate. That's the wrong reason. The only way it will work is if you and your ex have the strong feelings of confidence in each other that I described above. If you feel that strongly about the capability of the person you just divorced, then your children stand to benefit from this custody arrangement. But if there is any doubt whatsoever, your children would be better off if the two of you put your efforts toward other forms of custody arrangements and developed your own parental peace accord.

The important thing is to work to come to an agreement as to what is best for your children rather than have Judge No-Name do it for you. Again, you know your children better than the woman in the black robe. So whether you and your parenting partner come to an agreement of physical custody with scheduled visitation, or some form of joint custody, the important thing is that you work together to put the children first. Do what is best for them, not you. You know I'm going to say it…it's about the children, not you.

Notes and Thoughts

_____

_____

_____

_____

_____

_____

_____

_____

_____

_____

_____

_____

_____

_____

_____

_____

_____

_____

_____

_____

_____

_____

_____

_____

_____

7 | Visitation

This chapter will operate on the assumption that you are like most divorced parents, and one of you has physical custody of your children. Jurisdictions are fairly universal in holding that, absent a court order to the contrary, every non-custodial parent has a right to visitation. The fundamental purpose of this is quite simple. The court wants the child to have the opportunity to continue a healthy, growing relationship with both parents. In other words, the court believes it is in the child's best interest to have quality, uninterrupted time with the non-custodial parent in an effort to maintain or develop a balanced relationship. The problem is that this is the area where most divorced parents draw lines in the sand and commence battles.

It's A Right You Should Exercise

Most jurisdictions refer to these rights as *visitation rights* or *rights of visitation*. Interestingly enough, the majority addresses visitation as the right of the non-custodial parent, not the child. This is a bit of a dichotomy; although visitation is created with the best interest of the child in mind, it is considered the right of the non-custodial parent. This contradiction lends itself to the principle that visitation is only going to be in the best interest of the child if the non-custodial parent chooses to exercise his or her right.

All of this has created a great philosophical debate in among legal circles of various jurisdictions. If visitation is a right that a non-custodial parent may or may not choose to exercise, are there any *obligations* for the adult to exercise visitation with the minor child? It would seem that if visitation were created to provide children with balance in their lives, the non-custodial parent should have some obligation to meet this goal through the exercise of regular visitation. On the other hand, the more common argument is that the court awarded sole physical custody to one parent and that the custodial parent has physical custody at all times, except when the non-custodial parent elects to exercise his or her visitation rights.

"She was all packed and excited, waiting for her father to pick her up for the weekend, and he never showed." I wish I had a dollar every time I've heard that! The real issue in this situation is not that Dad didn't exercise visitation, but rather the kind of message it sends to a young child who is excited to spend the weekend with her Dad. And what can the non-custodial parent be thinking when he or she does this without so much as a phone call or explanation? This certainly isn't in the best interest of the minor child.

Once I represented a mother who could count on when the father wouldn't show to pick up the children for visitation. Whenever the father had reason to believe that the mother was planning to go out with friends, go on a date, or go on a short weekend getaway, something would mysteriously come up—something that required him to call and say, "Sorry, something came up, I just can't take the kids this weekend."

He had another game he would play if he found out she had plans *after* he had picked up the children. During the visitation, something would come up with the children that required him to contact her. If he couldn't reach her, he would later attempt to lay a guilt trip on her with comments like, "I can't believe you didn't tell me where you were going. The kids needed you!" Of course these comments were always made in the presence of their children. This nonsense bordered on child abuse, which I'll discuss in a later chapter.

The bottom line is that visitation is not some game of one-upmanship. If you do this, you are using your children as game pieces. Visitation is a right that every non-custodial parent should eagerly exercise. It is an opportunity to spend quality, one-on-one time with your children and learn about them while they learn from you. It is a time for fun, for making memories, and for reinforcing the parent-child bond that was threatened by the dissolution.

If you care about your children and are truly committed to the principles of *The Parental Peace Accord*, take the time to sit down with your parenting partner and jointly decide what is best for your children. Sure, if you can't do this, that guy in the black robe has already got it figured out, and he will hand down a court-ordered, standardized visitation schedule. But again, what does he know about your children? Does he know that they love spending Christmas Eve at their maternal grandmother's house? Does he know how much your children look forward to Dad's traditional breakfast, which he prepares on New Year's morning?

So sit down with your parenting partner and come to an agreement, or accord, on the type of visitation schedule that works best for your children. If you can't agree, you will always have the court's schedule to fall back on. But be flexible and put the kids first, not what is convenient for you. I have never known a court to interfere or find a couple in contempt of court for *agreeing* to a visitation outside of the schedule. Courts appreciate it when parents work together and create harmonious environments for their children.

Here's another suggestion. If you are the non-custodial parent, recognize that your ex-spouse is going to have a life. Recognize that as the custodial parent, there will be times when the need for a baby-sitter arises. If you're really committed to the primary concept of *The Parental Peace Accord*, ask the custodial parent if you can be offered the opportunity to spend time with the children when he or she needs a baby-sitter. This will give you and your children additional time together and will save the custodial parent baby-sitting fees. More importantly, it will send the message to your children that even though Mom and Dad are divorced, they still have two parents.

Pick Ups And Drop Offs

For those divorced parents who have trouble getting along, the exchange of the children when visitation is being exercised often creates the most stress. It doesn't have to be this way. Even if parents can't stand to look at each other, there are a few simple rules of engagement that can make for seamless, stress-free transfers.

I can't count the number of times clients have told me they took their children to the non-custodial parent who didn't show or wasn't home. Likewise, I've had a number of non-custodial clients tell me that the custodial parent wasn't home when the children were returned. There's an easy way to avoid this stress and inconvenience. Quite simply, whoever the children are scheduled to be with should be picking them up. If he or she doesn't show, the worst that could happen is that the parent with the children will have additional time with them and the peace of mind that comes from knowing they are safe.

In other words, if the non-custodial parent is exercising visitation, then the non-custodial parent should be responsible for picking the children up. This may be as simple as arriving at the custodial parent's residence or an agreed upon location. Using this practice, the worst that can happen is that the custodial parent has the children and the non-custodial parent either shows or doesn't show. This is still better than standing outside an unanswered door or sitting for an hour in a parking lot somewhere.

Likewise, when the visitation period is over, make it the custodial parent's responsibility to pick up the children. If the custodial parent arrives at the appointed time, great; if not, then the non-custodial parent gets to spend more time with the children and does not have to face the worry of getting the children back on time. This is a far better situation than having the custodial parent staring out a window, wondering when the children are going to show up. This is a very simple arrangement, but extremely effective.

Here's another rule of engagement to follow during the exercise of visitation. Never enter the other parent's residence unless invited. Seems simple enough, but it is amazing how many parents feel the need to go inside the residence of the other to see what's going on, what changes have been made to the house, and where did that new furniture come from. If parents are truly committed to the spirit of *The Parental Peace Accord,* this will be a non-issue, as those parents are not going to have a problem with their parenting partner stepping inside the door to pick up the children. However, for some, it may take time for that level of comfort to develop, and with others, it may never happen.

If you are the non-custodial parent, another good practice is to return the children with the same—and preferably clean—clothes they brought with them. Come on, be an adult. It's not that hard to quickly run a small load of laundry before the visitation period ends. It shows your kids that you care, and it shows them you respect their other parent. I know this seems trivial, but you cannot believe how many phone calls attorneys get on Sunday nights or Monday mornings with "She kept all of the clothes I sent with the children," or "He brought the kids back in the same clothes they were wearing when they left on Friday!" Parents committed to their parental peace accord will not have this issue.

Time: Quality vs. Quantity

The biggest shock to and the greatest concern for non-custodial parents is how much less time they have with their children, as compared to prior to the divorce. It had become routine to see the children every night before they went to bed and every morning before they went to school. Now the non-custodial parent may be looking at every other weekend and maybe one night during the week. It just doesn't seem fair. Well, it's not. But unfortunately, it is a common, negative side effect of dissolution. The question is, how are you going to deal with it?

The natural reaction for most new non-custodial parents is to over-plan. They want to make sure that the first time they spend time alone with the children since the divorce is a special occasion. So the non-custodial parent will plan an event agenda that will provide for an exciting, fun-filled weekend—one the children will never forget. Friday night we'll go out to dinner. Saturday morning we will get up and go shopping for new clothes. Saturday afternoon we'll go to the street fair. Saturday night we'll catch that new movie. Sunday morning we'll go out for brunch. Sunday afternoon we'll go bike riding. And Sunday night when the visitation is over, we will all be happy and smiling, pleased by how much we had accomplished in such a short period of time!

Uh, you might want to rethink this.

In most cases, what the children are really looking forward to is *you*. They love you, they miss you, and they are looking forward to spending time with you. The operative word here is *time*. If you plan a weekend like the one described above, there are going to be a lot of distractions during the time your children have to spend with you. This is not to say you shouldn't do those things with your children; it just means you should pace the activities and savor the time together.

Going out to dinner is great. Going to a movie is a wonderful thing to share. A street fair can be a blast. But it is extremely important that you allow your children to establish some normalcy and routine when they visit. Give them some quiet, quality one-on-one time. Ask them what happened to them over the last week or two. How is school? Who are they "hanging" with and what do they like to do? What was the best thing that happened to them since you saw them last? What was the worst thing?

Most importantly, listen to your children. They really do want to talk and share. The problem is most adults really don't listen to what children have to say. Adults are so busy interrupting to interject their own perspectives or beliefs on a particular subject that eventually, the children don't even bother. Give them the time while you have them. If they are talking to you, don't be reading the newspaper or watching television, while responding with the occasional "Uh-huh." Don't just *tell* them they have your undivided attention, *show* them. Put the newspaper down or turn the television off. This is precious, quality time when your children want to talk with you. They have a lot going on in their lives.

Of course, there is another extreme to this situation. I call it the smothering effect. This is the parent who bombards their children with questions and forces them to be subjected to the undivided attention that is being offered. Accept the fact that sometimes kids really don't want to talk. They're not in the mood. They're tired. They just want to be with you. Or they just want to be left alone and have some downtime. All of this is normal. Your job is to recognize this and make sure your child knows that when they are ready, you are always there for them to talk to about *anything*.

Without being intrusive, be a part of your children's lives. Don't always make them be a part of yours. If they want to have friends over, let them know that it is okay. It prevents them from having to say, "No, I can't get together this weekend because I have to go to my Dad's." More importantly, it gives you the opportunity to see the type of people they surround themselves with. I think one of the most important things in a child's development is their ability to pick the right friends.

Lastly, don't be afraid to mix it up with your children. One weekend you might go for a walk. Another weekend you might play a game they enjoy. And perhaps you will tell them in advance that another weekend is a mystery weekend. Give them clues. Tell them what clothes they'll need. Make it suspenseful. Then do something that is new and different. The object is to always allow your children to have happy, stable childhoods and to enjoy meaningful relationships with their parents.

Time, Not Money

Here's an interesting exercise. Think about your own childhood, and try to remember something that you really had fun doing. Seriously, stop reading, put this book down, and take a few minutes to think of things you remember as a child that were great fun.

Okay, I'm willing to make a bet that what you thought of was really something quite simple and inexpensive. I used to spend hours shooting basketballs at a basket bolted on a utility pole by the barn. My oldest son is now in his twenties. He's a good looking man standing about six-foot-three with an athletic build and a deep voice. I'm still caught off guard when he says, "Hey Dad, you remember how when I was little we always used to have a jigsaw puzzle on the table. We would spend hours trying to fit the pieces together. Man that was fun!"

Here's a child who had a passport at the age of ten, went on all kinds of trips, went to lots of movies, and went to tons of sporting events. But what he fondly remembers are those jigsaw puzzles! And even I have to admit, when I run across those old jigsaw puzzles in the closet, it sparks a flashback that brings a little smile across my face. This is probably why they have never made it to a garage sale.

Out of all of his years in sports, this same son's favorite memory is winning the fourth-grade basketball championship. He still has the team picture, and he's in his twenties. I have to ask myself as a parent, is this a great memory for him because the team won, or is it because I was coaching and it was something we were involved in together? As a parent, I think the reason is obvious and teaches a valuable lesson.

My youngest son was only three when his mother and I divorced. He is the more sensitive of the two and is always concerned about the feelings and thoughts of others. He still remembers us feeding the ducks when he was three years old. I find it amazing that out of all the childhood experiences he enjoyed, he remembers something as simple and inexpensive as feeding the ducks with his Dad. Why can't parents recognize that what our children really cherish is the quiet, quality time they spend with their parents?

I knew a divorced couple who had a son. The child was about eight years old at the time of the divorce, but I watched his development throughout the years. Both of his parents were very successful. His father owned his own business, which experienced tremendous growth due to his ability to recognize an opportunity and negotiate a good deal. His mother was a successful executive who was well-known throughout influential business and social circles. Both parents were very driven and enjoyed extremely active business and social lives.

They loved their son dearly and provided him with everything. He had a sporty new car, great looking clothes, travel opportunities, and the best seats at concerts and sporting events. He was good-looking, a fair athlete, and made good grades. But for some reason, I never felt that he was that happy. He was always polite and friendly, but it seemed as though he had developed a certain reserve and never allowed himself to open up or be vulnerable.

I often wondered if he would have traded all of the material things he had received for an invitation from his father to just go out in the yard and pass the football. I wonder if he would have traded some of the finer things in life just to have some quiet one-on-one time with his mother. It seemed they gave him everything except their time, and that is what he probably wanted the most. We forget that a daughter would love to just go for a walk with Mom, or how much a son would enjoy sitting by a campfire with Dad. This couple was so busy getting ahead in their own life and providing for themselves and their son that they forgot to give him the most important gift of all—time.

This young man has graduated from college now and has started to work with a local company. He lives in the same city as his divorced mother and father, but rarely sees them. How sad. There is a lesson to be learned here.

Visitation provides a wonderful opportunity for divorced parents who subscribe to the principles of *The Parental Peace Accord* to work together and show their children that they still have two parents who love them very much. It gives non-custodial parents an opportunity to spend some very special quality time with their children. It gives custodial parents a breather from the day-to-day responsibilities of being a single parent. More importantly, it allows the children to have a close, meaningful relationship with each parent— relationships they deserve.

Notes and Thoughts

_____

_____

_____

_____

_____

_____

_____

_____

_____

_____

_____

_____

_____

_____

_____

_____

_____

_____

_____

_____

_____

_____

_____

_____

_____

_____

_____

_____

_____

_____

8 | It's Called Child Abuse

Okay, let me just warn you up front that this chapter deals with an area that I don't tip-toe around with because I have no tolerance for it, nor should anyone else. You should also know that I have a pretty broad definition of child abuse. True, the dictionary defines abuse as "to hurt or injure by maltreatment." However, I define child abuse as anything that is detrimental to the health and well-being of the child; physically, mentally or emotionally.

In short, I feel that child abuse can take many forms. It can be the traditional horror of physical and/or sexual abuse. It can also take place in the form of verbal abuse, neglect, rejection, mind games, and even indifference. So, if you are engaged in any of these activities, stop it, and stop it now. There is no justification for this behavior.

Physical And Sexual Abuse

Let's start with the worst, physical and sexual abuse. Even though sexual abuse certainly qualifies as physical abuse, I refer to them separately. Physical abuse includes everything from locking children in closets, to beating them, or to inflicting physical torture and pain. It is hard to imagine that any parent could engage in this conduct, especially with the child they brought into the world. Unfortunately, it happens thousands of times a day, usually unnoticed and unreported.

Sexual abuse has to be the worst kind of physical abuse. To rob a young person of his or her sexuality and jeopardize his or her chance of a normal, healthy, adult relationship is incomprehensible. The emotional scarring caused by this form of abuse often never goes away. Again, it happens more frequently than people think, again often unnoticed and unreported.

The frustrating thing is that the people who engage in this deplorable behavior are not the ones reading this book. I'm assuming that you're reading this because you care deeply for your children, and you want what is best for them. These are not the feelings shared by those who engage in the physical and sexual abuse of children.

Physical and sexual abuses are zero-tolerance issues. As a parent, you have a duty to protect your child from this harm, regardless of who might be the perpetrator. If you suspect your child is being subjected to this behavior, it is your responsibility to have a calm, rational, non-hysterical discussion with your child. It is your responsibility to thoroughly investigate the issue and to be sure there is no mistake. After all of this, if your suspicions are confirmed, it is imperative that you contact the proper authorities. Your failure to act on this makes you guilty of child abuse also. In fact, to address this issue, many jurisdictions have incorporated "Failure to Report" crimes in their criminal codes.

As an aside, this is a touchy area. If you don't act, it's harmful for your child. If you do act, and you're wrong, that could also be harmful. If you're like the mother I described in Chapter Six and have made intentionally false allegations, then you are a miserable parent with no regard for your child and you should serve time. (I know, I need to quit holding back and tell you how I really feel.)

Neglect and Rejection

Neglect and rejection are two additional forms of abuse which may not seem as extreme as the aforementioned types, but they can also be very devastating. As hard as it is to understand, some parents throw away the relationships with their children as a part of throwing away their relationships with their spouses. I am saddened by the number of times I have seen a parent just disappear from a child's life after a dissolution. Some of these parents justify this by claiming it is too painful to see "the child they love so much." Others have an enormous desire to move on with their lives and feel that their children cannot be part of that process.

In most cases, this is nothing more than selfish hogwash. For parents to say that they can't be in their children's lives because they love them so much and it is just too painful is nonsense. These parent need to quit focusing on *their* feelings and consider their children's feelings instead. Think of what a child is going through emotionally when he has two parents that he loves; a divorce occurs, and now one of those parents is gone, out of his life forever. If you're that parent, you are neglecting your child and instilling feelings of rejection. The child doesn't see your pain. The child is trying to figure out what they did that was so wrong that it made you not love them or want to see them anymore. This creates a continuing emotional turmoil for the child.

I can tell you from firsthand childhood experience that there is no worse feeling for a child to feel than that of rejection. It is one thing for your children to feel like they are rejected by their peers, people they *thought* were their friends. It is quite another thing, and much more devastating, if your children feel rejected by you, their parent. As a parent, your child looks to you for protection and security. You have to be the one constant in his or her life, one who can always be depended upon. You have to be that one person in life: When all else fails, they know they can come to you and you'll be there. Now, imagine what it would be like if that was the person who rejected you. It would make a child's emotional world come tumbling down around them.

Need some examples of things you can say to make your child feel rejected? If your stomach can take it, try these on for size. "You'll never amount to anything!" "You're worthless, just like your father!" "You're a whore, just like your mother!" "What was I thinking when I said I wanted custody?" "You know, you're lucky I let you come and visit here." "I can see why nobody likes you." "Damn, I'll be glad when you're old enough to leave."

The list goes on and on. It may seem hard to believe that parents would say these kinds of things to their children, but I can tell you it is true. Any lawyer or judge involved in family law can tell you it is true and add more to the list. Imagine a child on the receiving end of these comments! For a child to hear these words from a person with whom they are so vulnerable is cruel. It's called child abuse.

There is another form of rejection that I need to discuss; I call it "tacit rejection." Tacit because it is rejection implied by or inferred from a parent's actions. We've all seen it. This is the parent who exercises visitation because he or she feels like it's an unwanted obligation. The visitation time is spent doing nothing, and the parent totally ignores the child. This parent is just waiting for the time to be up so that the child can be returned to the custodial parent. There is no conversation, no "How's school?" no nothing. I've heard children describe this rejection by saying, "Oh, my Dad doesn't really want to see me, he just does it because he has to." It's rejection. It's another form of child abuse.

Emotional Abuse

When taking an objective look at the emotional impact divorced parents can have on their children, we have to go back to the primary principle of *The Parental Peace Accord*; it's not about me, it's about the children.

I will never forget a father I represented who would not allow his children to have any pictures of their mother in their rooms. He told me he informed his children, "I divorced your mother, and I really don't want any memories of her in my house." I guess I kind of went off on him and asked him if he was crazy or just an idiot. He was confused by my reaction. I said, "Hey, Bill, how would you feel if someone told you that you couldn't have any pictures of your mother? This is exactly what you're doing to your son and daughter. And by the way, what are you going to do, have your little girl get plastic surgery? She looks just like her mother. Are you saying that she is not welcome in your house because when you look at her she reminds you of your ex-wife?" He finally got it.

What is important to remember here is that *you* divorced the other parent, not your child. Your child still loves that person just as much as he loves you and that person is still very much a part of his life. You are being selfish and unfair if you do not acknowledge this. I'm not saying the picture of your ex has to be hanging in your living room over the fireplace, but certainly your child should be allowed pictures of his other parent in the privacy of his own bedroom. It cuts both ways; your children should also be allowed to display pictures of you at the other parent's home. Now, you don't have a problem with that, do you?

Here's one that blows me away. One parent takes the child to an extracurricular activity, such as a play, concert, or ball game, but doesn't allow the child to go over and talk to the other parent. Apparently, this parent believes that since the child is in his or her custody during visitation time, the other parent is either invisible or doesn't exist. If you do this, you're being really stupid.

Think of what an uncomfortable position you're putting your child in. Instead of instructing your child to stay with you, or steering your child away from the other parent, you should allow the child to relish in the fact that both parents care enough to be there. The two people who mean the most to the child have come out for this event, and you're asking or demanding him or her to ignore one half of that equation. You may not be married, but you should always remember that your child has two parents. By the way, the same applies to grandparents who come to these events. Don't deny your child opportunities to feel special and loved. That kind of denial is harmful, and it's abusive.

Here's one that landed in my law office. Mom cheated on Dad and ran off with the kids to live with another man. The situation presented all the ingredients for an ugly divorce, which it was. In the end, Mom gets custody and remarries. Dad gets very liberal visitation because Mom really wants to have as much time as she can to develop her new marriage. Dad is a good father and loves spending all the visitation time with his children. He only has one rule. The children are not allowed to mention their mother's name in his house. By this time, the kids are pretty convinced that both of their parents are a little loony.

Of course we can understand the hurt and betrayal the father feels toward his children's mother. But in the end, this situation is really no different than that regarding the pictures. True, your ex may no longer be a major part of *your* life now, but your ex will always be your child's other parent. Think of what your reaction would be if you heard that your children were not allowed to mention your name in your ex-spouse's home. Just doesn't seem right, does it? That's because it's not.

Another situation along this same line of thought is telephone calls. Too many times I have heard of divorced or divorcing parents who will not allow their children to make phone calls to the other parent. The justification is "this is my time." This kind of reasoning may make sense to you, but it is totally confusing to your child. Yes, it's true that sometimes kids may want to use the phone to play one parent against the other. But if this is what is being done, acknowledge it with your children and tell them you won't allow it. However, this does not equate to forbidding them to call their other parent when they're with you.

Mind Games

I can't tell you the number of divorces I've sat through in which the parents behaved more childishly than the children. Unfortunately, it is often these same parents who engage in the practice of mind games. Oh, you know what I'm talking about. This occurs when a parent says or does some seemingly innocuous thing with a clear, underlying message or hidden agenda. The sad thing is that when parents do this, it is not fair play because the playing field between parent and child is not level. Sure, our teenagers think they know more than us about almost anything, but when it comes to judgmental statements, our children place a lot of weight on what we say and believe, regardless of their age.

There was a father in one of my divorces that was really nothing more than a couch potato. He would sit in front of the television for hours on end, watching ball games during his visitation time. The man just didn't have any motivation. Whenever his kids wanted to do something, he would make some seemingly sincere comment like, "Aw, I would love to do that, but unfortunately I have to pay your mom so much child support that I just don't have the money to do it." Another favorite was "Man, I was hoping we could take a vacation to the beach this year, but after paying child support to your mother, I just don't have the money. I'm sorry."

Well, at least he got the last part right. He is sorry. He is a sorry excuse for a father. Even if what he was saying were true, which in this case it wasn't, there was no need to put it in the context of child support payments. The only reason to do so is to play mind games with the children and create either sympathy for Dad or resentment for Mom. It would have been just as easy to simply say, "I would love to do that, but I just can't afford it right now." But then, that statement wouldn't get across the underlying meaning or hidden agenda, would it?

Just as bad was a mother I represented who would go on and on to her children about how tough it was to be a single mother. Being a single parent *is* tough. That's not the problem. The problem was how she used that fact to play mind games with her children. For years, she was extremely bitter toward her ex-husband. And for years her children would constantly hear statements like, "Your Dad is pretty fortunate to have a lot of free time to have a social life. It must be nice." Another often heard and seemingly innocent statement was "Oh, I don't think there are too many men out there who would be interested in a woman with two children"

These little mind games had two different effects on her children, and both were negative. Over the years, her son began to feel that all Mom did was whine, complain, and live her life as a victim. Over those same years, the daughter was made to feel that she was really in the way and her Mom's life would have been much happier if she hadn't had kids. Although Mom's mind games may have had the ulterior motive of gaining sympathy for herself and creating resentment toward her children's father, this is certainly not what occurred.

Okay, here's my last example of stupidity, uh, I mean mind games. I knew of a non-custodial father (we'll call him "Don") who probably did everything wrong that a parent could do regarding the relationship with his daughter. Even though he never did much to set a good example, his little girl adored him. She was a Daddy's girl, and no matter how inappropriate his behavior was in the post-dissolution environment, she still loved her Daddy. Her Mom would never speak ill of Don in her daughter's presence because she knew how much the little girl cared about her Daddy.

As the daughter got older, she began to realize that her father wasn't always fair. When she became a teenager she had even less tolerance for his boorish behavior. Eventually, there was a complete breakdown between the two, and she told her father she didn't want to visit him anymore. He told her that was fine by him. The father made no attempt to reconcile the relationship—no phone calls, no birthday presents, no Christmas presents. Now, you might say the daughter was just as guilty for not trying to reconcile, but let's not forget Don is the parent; his daughter is the child. Besides, it gets worse. Although he didn't get her a birthday present, he did send her a birthday card that was signed, "Happy Birthday, Don." Not Daddy or Dad. Don.

For the daughter, the signing of a birthday card in such a way was the emotional equivalent of a slap in the face. The message this little mind game sent was meaner than any child should have to experience. It is hard to believe that there are parents who can ignore the vulnerability of their children and engage in this kind of conduct. Playing these types of mind games with your children isn't just mean, it's child abuse.

If you play mind games with your children, then you are lying to your children. I say this because you are making a statement, true or not, that is not being made for the reason and purpose for which it appears. Any time you engage in this conduct you are playing a game in which there can be no certainty of the outcome. In fact, in my observations, it usually backfires. When it backfires, it would be easy to say, "Good, they got what they deserve," but unfortunately, it is usually the children who get hurt the most.

If you want to subscribe to the principles of *The Parental Peace Accord*, I strongly encourage you to skip the mind games and to be truthful with your children. It is okay for them to see that you are human and not living on top of some pedestal. You can verbalize your insecurities without sabotaging you ex-spouse. If you allow yourself to play mind games with your children, no matter how tempting it is, you are not only sabotaging your ex-spouse; you are sabotaging your children's other parent. This can be very dangerous and have negative— even disastrous—results.

Indifference

Indifference may be one of the more obscure forms of child abuse, but to me, it's still child abuse. In short, indifference is when your words or lack of words and actions or lack of actions convey to your child that you just don't care. It's kind of like neglect, but without the assertiveness. These are the parents who will hardly ever respond to anything at all, and if they do, it might be with that worn out response of "whatever."

Indifference can come in many varied forms. It can be the non-custodial parent who never calls the children just to see what's new. It can be the parent who never shows up to or stays at any of the child's sporting events or other extracurricular activities. It can be the custodial parent who forgets to pick the children up after a visitation. It can be a parent who forgets their child's birthday.

The very worst is the parent who just doesn't have anything to say to their children. I find it unbelievable that a parent can be riding in a car or sitting down to dinner with their child and have nothing to say—complete silence. I'm not saying that parents should jabber on endlessly, and I'm not saying that there is anything wrong with silence. What I'm referring to are those parents who never engage their children in conversations to ask them how school is going or how they like their new coach. An absence of these kinds of simple questions shows a lack of involvement or interest. This lack of involvement or interest constitutes indifference. Indifference is a surefire way to make your children feel unloved and unimportant.

In summary, there is no room, need, nor any justification for child abuse, no matter what form it takes. More importantly, there should be no tolerance for it. A stranger or a peer will knock us on our cans if we are abusive toward them, but our children trust us and are therefore vulnerable to the way we treat them. They deserve your best behavior.

Notes and Thoughts

9 | Establish the Routine

This chapter is really about creating stability for your children. It is imperative that parents agree as soon as possible on a routine for their children. During or after a divorce, it is quite natural for children, of any age, to have feelings of anxiety and detachment. Their entire world has been thrown into a tailspin, and they feel they have no control over what's going on around them.

Two people they love are at each other's throat. They don't know where they are going to live. They don't know what their future is with their parents. They don't know what their future is with their friends. And how did this happen? Divorce is something that only happened to other kids. For them, life sucks.

So while you're all wrapped up in your own emotions, turmoil, and insecurities, your kids are in a living hell emotionally. What are you going to do about it? If you're any kind of parent at all, you can't ignore it. At the same time, there are so many issues going on right now in terms of the divorce, such as living arrangements, property division, custody, visitation, and work, that there just doesn't seem to be enough time to be the emotional support system your children need now.

Tough. You'll get no sympathy here. You don't have a choice. Your kids didn't ask for this, and you have a responsibility to provide them with a stable and happy childhood. It's time to get your emotions under control and get on your game as to being a good parent. Nobody said it was going to be easy, and nobody said you weren't going to make mistakes. Just remember, the entire foundation of *The Parental Peace*

Accord process is to put the children first. If you do that, trust me, everything else will fall into place.

Creating Stability

What your children really need right now is some stability in their lives. You and your parenting partner are the people in the best position to provide that. Step one: you need to have honest conversations with your children. This whole honesty thing is discussed pretty extensively in the next chapter. Step two: one of the best tools you can use to achieve stability for your children is to establish routines.

Why routines? Routines inherently create expectations. Expectations that are consistently met create stability. Right now your children are living in a world of unknowns. Their world is upside down. They really don't know what's coming. When you establish routines that you both adhere to, it will inject a sense of normalcy in an unfamiliar, emotional situation.

I need to make an apology up front, prior to delving into this discussion. A law practice doesn't take an attorney into the homes of clients very often. As a result, it is difficult for me to give very many examples of establishing routines other than my own personal experiences. Sorry about that, but I think you'll get the point.

As a child, my orphanage experiences were not that good. But one thing that made it bearable was the established routine. Obviously, I was too young to realize this was going on, but somewhere down the line, someone in the California Department of Social Services figured routine would give a bunch of mixed-up kids some stability. Every morning at exactly the same time, breakfast would be ready in the dining hall. Every night at exactly the same time it was lights-out. Every Thursday we would exchange our dirty clothes for clean clothes. Every Sunday, family and friends would visit many of the children. Not an easy situation for kids, but this certainly exhibits the positive impact routines can have.

When discussing routines in a dissolution setting, the first and most obvious topic that comes to mind is visitation. This was discussed pretty thoroughly in Chapter Seven, but in the context of routines, it is important that you understand the significance of being consistent in visitation. Quit thinking about visitation consistency in terms of *your* reliance and expectancies. Instead, think of how important it is that *your children* are able to expect and rely on visitation with a parent. This gives them something they can count on—a routine that gives them a sense of stability.

It is equally important that if you and your parenting partner are required to make some change in the visitation schedule, it is not enough that you communicate that to each other; you need to make sure you communicate it to your child along with an explanation of why. Children should not be the last to know about visitation issues. Remember, you're trying to create stability.

Holidays are also a great time to establish routines that create stability. It is very likely that there are traditions or visits to relatives that used to be a regular part of a holiday routine. If it is feasible, you should try to maintain as many of those as possible. If the whole family always went to your parents' house for the holidays, or your parents came to yours, try to maintain that tradition. While it may not seem like a big deal to you, and it may require a lot of effort on your part, you would be surprised as to how much that traditional routine gives your children a sense of stability.

As I've mentioned, my sons and I are movie buffs. We have always had a tradition of watching *Christmas Vacation*, starring Chevy Chase, every Christmas Eve before we go to bed. Even though we've seen this movie countless times, we continue to belly laugh at the experiences of the "Griswold Family Christmas." I realize that as my sons grow older and establish their own lives, there may come a time when this tradition comes to an end. But I also wouldn't be surprised if in the years to come, I find myself surrounded by grandchildren on Christmas Eve, and one of my sons says, "Hey, you know what we have to do? It's time to watch *Christmas Vacation!*"

Here's a tradition you won't believe. I have often teased my ex-wife that where I really got screwed in the divorce was the loss of a great cook. She's one of those Italians who is blessed with a natural talent for the culinary arts. Each year on Father's Day, she comes to my house and prepares an incredible dinner for all of us. Now I admit, as a result of our commitment to the principles of *The Parental Peace Accord*, our post-divorce relationship is probably an exception, rather than the norm, for most divorced couples. But trust me, she doesn't do this because she can't wait to see me or wants to fill my stomach. She does it because she sees, as do I, how much happiness that tradition brings to our sons. They like knowing their parents can get along and be civil to each other. And as strange as it may sound, that once-a-year tradition gives them a sense of stability. So once a year, I feel an obligation to subject myself to this wonderful food for the benefit of my sons. That's my story, and I'm sticking to it.

Sometimes routines that don't seem to have a direct impact on the children do, in fact, contribute to stability. For instance, parenting partners should always make it a routine to exchange reports and information with each other. This may include report cards, medical reports, practice schedules, or even a letter from school. If this is done, each of the parents is in the loop as to what is going on in their child's life, and that will go a long way in providing your child with some needed stability.

I even recommend this information-sharing routine to parents who don't get along. A parent may ask me, "Why send this stuff to him? He doesn't look at it or do anything about it anyway." Nevertheless, you have nothing to lose by taking the time and effort to drop the information in the mail. The worst that can happen is nothing. The best that can happen is that your ex-spouse and child find themselves with something to talk about.

Another thing I can't stress enough when discussing routines is how much the little things count toward establishing some level of normalcy and stability. When I was first divorced and my children were still young, every night before bed, all three of us would say our prayers together. It's amazing how much you can learn about what your child is thinking when you're saying your prayers together. Not only did it help me, but it played a big part in establishing some stability in their young lives.

Now here's one that, to this day, still blows me away. Talk about the little things! When my sons and I moved into our current house, we sat down at the kitchen table to eat. No big deal. The only thing is that our table has six chairs, and there were only three of us. We just sat down. However, the next time we sat down to eat and every time thereafter, we each sat in the same chair! Not a big deal, and it probably happens at every family table, but I find it pretty interesting that even to this day, when the boys come home, or even if they sit down at the table by themselves, they always sit in the same chairs. Again, don't ever underestimate the small things. Now that they're grown, I've often wondered what would happen if I sat in one of their chairs. I can only assume that mass confusion would follow and the world, as we know it, would probably come to an end.

These routines don't have to be difficult to be effective. It may be something as simple as setting a bedtime, going to church, or establishing discipline. I have a theory about this. It is fairly common for children to complain about having to go to bed at a certain time. And sometimes, they really don't want to get up and go to church. Lastly, they certainly don't look forward to being punished. But I believe that subconsciously they have positive feelings associated with the security and stability of knowing the routines, even if they don't like them. As the comedian Dennis Miller says, "That's just my opinion; I could be wrong."

In terms of routines, don't forget that some of them can be fun. If you're going to your son's baseball games throughout the season, certain rituals like putting the folding lawn chairs in the trunk, icing down Gatorade in the cooler, and stopping for ice cream, can become part of the routine. If your daughter plays basketball, you may find that putting her hair in a ponytail, giving her a hug after the game, and discussing the play-by-play on the way home are rituals that become part of a stabilizing routine.

Create New Routines

Don't be afraid to create new routines. This is something that you and your children can develop together. Pick a theme and decide what you want to do. For instance, you might decide it would be cool to give something back to the community. So you resolve to engage in some kind of charitable activity once a month. Maybe one weekend you donate the toys they have outgrown to a charitable organization. Maybe you take that elderly widow from church a cake that you and the kids baked. Perhaps you can collect all the old books in the house and give them to the local orphanage (or children's home, as they are called in some areas). Not only are you creating a new and different tradition, but your children get to experience the positive feelings which stem from doing something for somebody else.

I know one single mother who does a really cool thing with her daughters. She will pick a day and declare it "Katie Day" or "Kelsey Day." This day is a day that is focused and directed one hundred percent toward that particular daughter. It may involve shopping, going to a movie, going out to eat, cooking her favorite meal, or just taking a drive. This little routine always comes as a surprise, gives the girls something to look forward to, and makes them feel pretty special.

A similar exercise is to have a "Girls' Weekend" or "Guys' Weekend." This can consist of a trip out of town, going to a game, a camping trip, or a shopping trip. You and your kids can have a lot of fun planning these weekends. The more planning you let them do, the more fun it is for them. After you do this a couple of times, it becomes a routine that creates a fun bonding experience. Who said routines have to be boring?

If the word *routine* is getting in the way of your creativity, use the word *tradition*. You and your children can have a lot of fun creating new traditions. It may be some annual event that you do together. I know one father who takes his son to a Chicago Cubs game every year. It is routine in the sense that they drive to Chicago the same way, stay at the same hotel, sit in the same seats, and the Cubs lose. But it is a routine that they each look forward to with great anticipation.

When my oldest son graduated from high school, we decided that we would take a "Graduation Trip" and spend a week together in Florida. We decided we were going on this trip as buddies, not father and son. The rule was, "What happens in Florida, stays in Florida." It was really a pretty innocent week, but my son and I had a blast. I admit I was feeling a little guilty leaving my other son behind, but that feeling went away when I realized how much he was looking forward to *his* Graduation Trip.

I encourage you to think about special routines and traditions that you and your children can enjoy. Find something that you both enjoy and that you can do together. If you both like basketball, maybe it's a regular pick-up game of one-on-one. If you and your daughter enjoy shopping, maybe you set up an annual shopping spree in another city. Or perhaps you and your kids will find mutual fun in great bonding activities, such as camping, boating, bike riding, or hiking. This routine involvement and activity not only creates stability for your children, but strengthens the bonds of a relationship that will last the rest of your life. In short, get involved, be a part of your child's life, and make that a routine.

Here's a different twist on the subject of routines. Not only do your children benefit from the stability routines can create, but you can too. I know a family that consists of a mother, her four adult daughters, and her daughters' children. Two of the daughters are divorced, one is widowed, and the fourth has never been married. Almost every Sunday these grown daughters go to their mother's home for a midday meal.

In addition to the adult daughters, it is not uncommon to see their children, current spouses, boyfriends, and significant others also in attendance. It sometimes gets to be quite a crowd, but it happens every Sunday. It is a routine that has gone on for years. I would suggest to you that without them realizing it, this routine has played a big part in their lives by giving all of them the stability to cope with divorces, breakups, deaths, and a few other challenges life has thrown at them.

I have had the good fortune to attend a few of these Sunday dinners, and you would be amazed by the amount of warmth, happiness, and energy exuded during this Sunday ritual. It's not planned, forced or expected; it just naturally occurs out of routine. Sisters are joking with each other, cousins are watching television or "hanging" together, and when the aroma of a home-cooked meal hits them, they can't wait to eat. It's as if every Sunday was a holiday. I truly admire this family.

Years ago, Sunday family dinners were pretty common. During the week, families actually sat down and ate together in the evenings and discussed the day's events. Today, we live in such a fast-paced society that eating out is the norm and eating at home is the exception. That's too bad. I think we may be underestimating the impact that evening meals played in holding families together. It's something to think about.

Now, while you're busy thinking of routines that will work for you and your family, here's another piece of advice. Try not to screw up the routines that are already an established part of your child's life. Remember that your child has a life with their other parent, and there are probably some pre-existing routines. These routines are just as important to your child's stability as the ones they have or create with you. In other words, try to plan things in such a way that routines can be maintained for your child with both parents. Once again, it's about your child, not you.

There's an interesting thing about routines. Many people connect a negative connotation with the word *routine*. To them, it brings to mind thoughts of everything mundane. People feel that if something is routine, it must be uneventful, boring, and a chore.

The fact is routines have a lot to offer. They provide a certain level of expectation; when that level of expectation is met, a sense of security and stability is produced. They also create and enforce tried-and-true procedures. For example, an aircraft pilot goes through the routine of a pre-flight checklist. He or she does it the same way each and every time. Why? Because it is a proven procedure used to avoid pitfalls. It gives the pilot a sense of security and stability by knowing that the aircraft is prepared for flight.

It's Not That Hard

That is what this chapter is about—providing your children with a sense of security and stability. Routines, whether large or small, play a big part in allowing your children to live in a world where expectations are met. There has never been a time in your children's lives when the stability and security provided by routines have been needed more. The beauty of establishing routines is that while it is not difficult, it is so beneficial. Equally significant is the fact that in comparison to the more elaborate routines, the minor ones are just as effective, if not more so, at creating stability.

Whether it is something as simple as bedtimes, going to church, curfews, or sitting in the same chair at the kitchen table, these routines will become the hidden support system for your child's emotional well-being. Your children may resist or object to some of these traditions, but you're the parent, and if you feel it is important, then you've got to stand by your guns and do what's best for them—whether they see it or not.

One of the easiest ways to accomplish the use of routines is to take a careful look at your children's pre-divorce lives. What was a part of their day-to-day routines? When was their bedtime? What time was curfew? What did they eat for breakfast? Start with the simple things and work from there.

Likewise, take a good look at family traditions. What did we do at Christmas? Where did we go on vacation? Which events did the kids really enjoy? Many of these can—and should—continue.

I have one last suggestion. Some traditions just can't be continued because your ex-spouse was a significant part of them, or the memory of your ex may be counterproductive in regard to what you're trying to accomplish with your children. In those difficult instances, you will have to take an entirely different approach. When in doubt, always go back to honesty. Don't be afraid to talk to your children and acknowledge that a particular tradition just won't work anymore. But rather than being negative or morose about it, take a positive approach. Ask the kids to help you figure out a new tradition, one to replace the old one. "We can't do this, so what do you think we should do?"

This approach allows the children to play an active part in the solution instead of having it dictated to them by you. Their replacement tradition may require a bit more work or flexibility on your part, but give it a shot. Also, it is not uncommon for kids to be concerned about the loneliness of the parent they're not with, and this is perfectly natural. Instead of trying to cover it up, don't deny them their feelings. Let them know that if they want to call Mom or Dad, it's okay. That phone call may become a new routine. That's because it's about the kids, not you.

Notes and Thoughts

_____

_____

_____

_____

_____

_____

_____

_____

_____

_____

_____

_____

_____

_____

_____

_____

10 | Honesty: the <u>Only</u> Policy

Dan Sullivan, the founder of an executive coaching organization called The Strategic Coach®, once told me, "All progress begins with telling the truth." I believe this to be true in every aspect of our lives, be it business, friendships, emotions, or divorce recovery. It is natural for parents to want to protect their children, especially during something as traumatic as the dissolution of a marriage. It is also natural that in the course of protecting their children, parents will want their children to feel that everything is under control, physically and emotionally.

However, all things may not be under control, and that is also natural. What some parents don't get is that open, honest communication is the first step to recovery. Everyone knows that if a participant is going to address the group at an Alcoholics Anonymous meeting, the first words spoken are, "My name is _____, and I am an alcoholic." We've all seen it on television, and some have witnessed it firsthand.

What's the point? The point is that before the AA participant can move forward, he or she must acknowledge the truth for what it is; he or she is an alcoholic. The same principle of honesty can be applied to a dissolution environment. If you feel frightened, guilty, hurt, or alone, the first thing you need to do is acknowledge that feeling. Until you acknowledge the feeling, you can't deal with it. Some will be able to accomplish this on their own; others may need professional counseling to work through it.

It is amazing how many parents seem to be in a state of denial or avoidance after or during the dissolution of their marriage. I have represented many clients who made every effort to keep the fact they were divorced a secret. It was as if it was something that they or their children were not supposed to talk about. In some cases, it seemed they were not even supposed to talk about it with each other. It was a forbidden subject. Such an attitude will certainly prolong the time required to recover and move on from a divorce for both the parents and the children. If you're one of these parents, perhaps like AA, you need to look in the mirror and say, "My name is _____, and I am a divorced parent."

Vulnerability Can Be A Good Thing

Here's another thought. It's okay to be honest with your children. It's okay to let them know what you're feeling. I'm not suggesting you use your children as counselors or make your issues the primary focus to the extent that their emotional needs are overlooked. I'm simply saying that it is perfectly appropriate for you to acknowledge your feelings with your children. If done properly, this will let your children see that you are, in fact, human and that the circumstances you are putting them through are not pleasant for you either.

My sons have always put me up on what I call the "Dad pedestal." They see me as this strong personality, taking on the tough cases and pursuing the big business deals. I'll never forget one evening when they were young and the ink wasn't even dry on the Decree of Dissolution. I was having a rough night and was probably a little quieter and more somber than usual. My oldest son, at the ripe old age of seven, kept asking me what was wrong. Of course, I gave him the standard parental response, "Oh, nothing."

Being a chip off the old block that he is, he was relentless and kept inquiring. I finally said to him very quietly, "I'm just feeling kind of sad about the divorce your mom and I went through. Sometimes I feel like such a failure." He looked at me, gave me a hug, and said, "Dad, you're not a failure. I've got the best dad in the whole world, and I've got the best mom in the whole world. It's going to be okay."

At that very moment, after hearing this wise counsel from my seven year old, I felt instantly better. And he and I felt a personal bond that has never left us. I think that seeing the tower of strength he called Dad show emotional vulnerability made him feel closer to me. It showed him human frailty in a person whom he perceived to be bigger than life. It showed him honesty in its truest emotional form.

Sometimes parents and children have difficulty with verbally expressing their true feelings. There are certainly other ways of doing it. Although I feel I'm fortunate to have a pretty open, verbal dialogue with both of my sons, we will often write each other little notes. My youngest son is partial to notes and text messages, while my oldest seems to prefer cards and e-mail. Shortly after the experience I shared in the above paragraph, I received a Valentine's Day card from my oldest son who, as I said, was seven at the time. It showed a picture of his favorite Teenage Mutant Ninja Turtle and read, "You are my Valentine. You can lean on me." Okay, I admit it...I cried. I bought a frame for that card, and I still have it today.

My sons are seventeen and twenty-one at the time of this writing. It is still not uncommon for my youngest to send a text message to my cell phone that simply says, "I love you." Likewise, I will often leave notes, e-mails, voice mails, and cards for no reason other than to tell them how special they are and how much I love them.

The point is to make sure you understand how important it is for you to be emotionally honest with your children. Let them know how much they mean to you. Let them know how much you love them. It doesn't matter whether you tell them verbally, with a card, note, or e-mail—just let them know. They will always need to hear it, especially now.

It is also important to provide your children with encouragement any time the opportunity arises. If they make good grades, do well in sports, or contribute in some way, make it a celebration. Show your pride and let them see it. There is nothing more rewarding than for your child to receive a handwritten card from you that states, "I am so lucky. I'm glad I'm your dad. I love you!" This simple, emotionally honest statement can create an enormous amount of stability, self-esteem, and security in your child.

Being evasive is another practice parents will employ in an effort to "protect" their children. Unfortunately, most parents don't realize that their children can usually see right through this.

"Where are you going tonight, Mom?"

"Oh, I've got a meeting."

Good grief. Just be honest, and tell the poor kid you met this really nice guy at work who asked you out to dinner.

"You're not getting married to him, are you, Mom?"

Oh, no! This was what you were afraid of. You knew you shouldn't have listened to that Bailey guy and should have just told your child you had to go to a meeting. Now what will you do? How about saying, "Of course not, it's just dinner. Even Moms have to eat, right?"

As long as you are honest with your children, there shouldn't be too many emotional surprises for them to deal with. It's when you're not honest—whether it be in the form of outright lying or through evasiveness—that reality sneaks up on your kids when they least expect it. All of a sudden, something that could have been a non-issue is now a major topic that must be addressed in a potentially stressful environment.

Two-way Honesty

As you are honest with your children, you may discover a valuable by-product. When parents practice honest communication with their children, it is not uncommon for them to find their children engaging in more honest communication with them as well. And this is certainly a time in their lives when you need to know their honest feelings as they are also dealing with the emotions stemming from your marital dissolution. If you're lucky enough to experience this type of communication, nurture and reinforce this special part of your relationship with your child. It will last a lifetime.

Another important part of the honesty aspect is keeping your promises to your children. Sounds simple enough, huh? Unfortunately, it's not always that easy. Many times we, as parents, will promise our children something that for one reason or another just doesn't work out. For us it may not be that big of a deal, but to our children, certain reliances and expectations may have been created that are now unfulfilled.

"I promise we will be out of this apartment and in a new house by next year."

"I promise that you're going to like your new school."

You might want to use a little discretion in using that *promise* word around your children. To them it can be a word that means an unqualified commitment. I know a single mother, who is a great parent and who will go to great lengths to avoid using the *promise* word. Instead of telling her daughters, "I promise I'll pick you up at five o'clock," she consciously phrases her statement as "I should be there to pick you up at five o'clock." A little compulsive perhaps, but I think you get the point.

Painful Honesty

As long as we're discussing honesty and the need to carefully phrase things, there is another area we should discuss. How do we handle those tough questions that our children ask? You know, those short, two-ton questions, such as, "Mom, why did you leave Daddy?" Nothing like enjoying an ice-cream cone with your son and having him ask out of the clear blue sky, "Daddy, why did you and Mommy get divorced?"

These are not questions that should be ignored or brushed off with some evasive, rhetorical reply. Conversely, it's probably not a swell idea to tell your child, "Because your Dad is a lazy, womanizing, worthless drunk." Nor would it be appropriate to respond, "Because your Mom is a lunatic who should be committed, and I'd rather jump in quicksand than live with a whore like her." In your own mind, these things may be true, but there are better honest approaches to take with your children. Remember, you're talking about a parent they love, whether you do or not.

You might consider less abrasive but still honest statements such as, "You know, I thought your mom and I would be married forever, but we had just become so unhappy in our life together that something had to be done—even if it would be painful." I represented one mother who told her children, "Divorcing your father was the hardest decision I have ever made in my life, but after struggling with that decision for so long, I knew that it was the right decision for all of us. Your father loves you very much. Unfortunately, he is going through a lot of things in his life that only he can work out. He needs our support and prayers."

Now, I don't want to give anybody sugar-induced diabetes here, so let me be clear by saying that yes, there are times when brutal, painful honesty is appropriate. In situations of spousal abuse, especially abuse that the children have witnessed, it is important to tell your children, "That is not the way you treat someone you're married to, and you should never allow anyone to treat you that way. It is wrong, and it should never be tolerated!"

Likewise, if the children themselves have been abused, physically or psychologically, it is your responsibility to let them know they should not have been subjected to that type of behavior. I represented a husband in this situation, and he was very direct with his children and told them, "I love your mother very much, but we all know what was happening, and I have a responsibility to protect you from that kind of treatment. You are a good person and don't deserve to be treated that way. I love you, and I will always be here for you."

So how far do we take this honesty thing, anyway? Where do you draw the line between being honest and exposing your children to a level of emotional stress that they shouldn't have to endure? If you are truly committed to *The Parental Peace Accord* and its process, the best advice is to use your instincts as a loving and caring parent. You will know when you've crossed the line.

For example, I once represented a woman who was so steeped in self-pity that she was driving her children crazy, as well as me, her attorney. Her entire focus was on what the divorce was going to mean to *her*. She would continually express to her children that she didn't know what they were going to do or how they were going to survive. It wasn't so much that she was being painfully honest with her children as much as it was that she was seeking the pity and attention of everybody around her, including her children. It didn't matter who she was talking to; all she could talk about was how terrible her life was and how she just didn't know what she was going to do.

Okay, some people will handle the stress of a marital dissolution better than others. Some will truly need professional counseling to get through it. But children are not professional counselors. They have their own issues and cannot be the same pillar of strength for their parents that their parents need to be for them. In this case, instead of providing support for her children, she had induced such a state of fear and anxiety in her children about their future that one of them actually developed ulcers!

Children are children, and they deserve a stable childhood. Just because Mom and Dad are getting a divorce does not mean they, the children, cannot have a stable childhood. It is up to you to make sure that happens. Depending on their age, kids are usually pretty busy just trying to figure out life. The young ones are trying to learn the difference between right and wrong, and how to deal with that new big place called *school.* The older ones are trying to find out who they are and who among their peers are really their friends. In the middle of all of this, it is pretty hard for them to be the sole emotional support system for their parents, nor should this be asked of them.

Conversely, I once represented a father who was a real macho type and as strong as tempered steel. So strong in fact, that he never really took the time to be honest with himself or his children. Any time his children asked questions about the divorce or the subject arose, he summarily stated, "What's happened has happened. It's time to move on." What the hell does that mean? How does a twelve-year-old boy process that statement while struggling with the fact that the two people whom he loves and counts on the most just got divorced and decided to go their separate ways?

The result was very confused children who didn't understand why the divorce took place. They might have wondered if they were to blame. They might have had feelings of insecurity. Worst of all, they may have felt uncomfortable discussing their feelings with a parent who was unable to share his or her feelings honestly. That strong, iron persona may have been a stronger shell than the child felt he or she could penetrate. These kind of results were probably not intended by the parent, but they were still very real.

So now you're saying, "Bailey, all right, enough already! So how do you draw the line when it comes to honesty?" Gee, I'm glad you asked that. The answer to that very difficult question goes back to the basic principle of *The Parental Peace Accord*. It's not about you; it's about the children.

Within the contest of this book, the entire concept of honesty being the *only* policy is based upon what is best for your children. Your honesty has to stem from a need and a desire to help them, not yourself. That's the line. I cannot draw it any straighter, nor can I make it any clearer. Your children are vulnerable right now, and the honesty has to be for them, not you.

If you are making these "honest" statements about your ex-spouse or your current situation because it makes you feel better, then you're probably crossing the line. If your wife cheated on you, of course, it might make you feel good to call her names. If your husband was a drunk, it may be great therapy to remind your children of that. Then they know and remember that it was *his* fault the marriage didn't work out. The problem is that none of these so-called honest statements are serving your children's needs. If anything, it is probably doing more damage than good. You have crossed the line.

Surprisingly, you can cause just as much harm by not being honest enough. Those parents who are the strong, silent types will do it every time. They feel the way to show their children strength and stability is with a stiff upper lip. They believe this sends the message, "Everything is okay, and I'm not fazed by anything." These people are the same ones who never cry at funerals.

The reason this lack of honesty also crosses the line is because it deprives your children of the needed support that honesty can provide. It is an unintentional form of emotional abandonment. You may offer up the excuse that you haven't really had any discussions with your children because they have never brought up the divorce. Who are you kidding? If you are portraying this strong, unemotional personality, just how comfortable do you think your kids are going to be when they come up to you and say, "Hey Dad, I'm kind of wigged out about this whole thing. Can we talk about the divorce?"

As parents, we all know that kids don't always know what's best for them. That's why they have parents. Specifically, when they feel insecure and confused, they don't really understand the need to discuss it. Their lack of understanding seems to exist regardless of age. In short, you can't always wait for them to initiate honest discussion. Sometimes you need to pose gentle, non-intrusive inquiries such as "Hey, I realize this is a pretty stressful time for all of us. Are you okay? Is there anything you want to talk about or ask me? If not, and you change your mind, I'm always here."

Make honest statements to your children that are in their best interest, and you won't have to worry about crossing the line. If you do this and truly have their best interest at heart, you will find that using this type of communication creates support and stability for your children.

Instead of referring to a child's father as a drunk—which he or she probably already knows—refer to him as an individual who has a few challenges in his life to work through. Instead of maintaining a façade of strength and silence, show your children that you understand their insecurities and anxieties because you are experiencing some of them yourself. Instead of lecturing them on what they *should* be feeling, be there for them and listen to what they *are* feeling. Instead of giving them all the answers, help them to discover the answers for themselves.

Nobody said this honesty thing was going to be easy. It takes a lot of courage and thought. It also requires you to be a little bit vulnerable, which—if you're like me—doesn't always come easily. It also requires sincerity; this isn't something you want to fake. The good news is that like most things, the more you practice it, the easier it becomes. The better news is that you will be providing your child with support and stability that is very much needed at times like these. The great news is that in the process, you will probably build a bond with your child that will last a lifetime.

Notes and Thoughts

_____

_____

_____

_____

_____

_____

_____

_____

_____

_____

_____

_____

_____

_____

_____

_____

_____

_____

_____

_____

_____

_____

_____

_____

_____

_____

_____

_____

_____

_____

_____

_____

_____

_____

_____

_____

_____

_____

_____

_____

_____

_____

_____

_____

_____

_____

11 | Doing the Right Thing

W hether you are in the middle of a divorce, or just out of one, or years down the road, there will always be those times when your emotions threaten to take over. When this happens, you will be required to do a little "gut check" to monitor your behavior. During years of family law practice, I have seen parents engage in conduct that would shock them, were they to hear about someone else engaging in the exact same conduct. So how does this happen? Quite simply, it is often difficult for us to control our emotions, and when we lose that control, we are capable of doing some pretty bizarre things.

In a legal context, there are laws in many jurisdictions that reflect and recognize this lost control of emotions. For instance, the "self-defense" argument in a criminal trial represents a person's reasonable belief that he or she was in a life-threatening situation or one that threatened bodily harm. This person, in fact, may not have been in a truly life-threatening situation, although at the time, it may have been reasonable for him or her to believe so. A better example in criminal trials might be the "heat-of-the-moment" mitigating circumstances argument, whereby a person's emotions at the instant of the event contribute to the outcome.

So when you are in a divorce or post-divorce situation that deals with something as close to the heart as your children, how do you keep those emotions in check? I would suggest you begin by recognizing that emotions are reactions to an event or situation. *Webster's Dictionary* defines emotion as "a strong feeling about somebody or something." A second definition given is "agitation or disturbance caused by strong feelings." In other words, these strong feelings are caused by our *reactions* to somebody or something.

In the business world, company leaders know and live by the rule that it is better to be proactive than reactive. Accordingly, successful executives work hard to anticipate undesirable situations before they occur, then proceed in a direction that may prevent the situation altogether. In the corporate environment, this practice is often called "risk management and avoidance." Those organizations that live by this practice are usually the ones that are able to survive challenging times in a competitive business environment.

I would submit to you that a similar approach can be used to make *The Parental Peace Accord* a more effective tool for you and your ex-spouse. Let's face it: there are plenty of opportunities for awkward and uncomfortable situations to create reactionary emotions during a divorce or a post-dissolution relationship. So you have a choice: are you going to be *proactive* or *reactive* to those situations?

Okay, for the rest of this discussion I am going to operate under the assumption that you gave the correct answer to the last question by choosing to be proactive in the peace accord relationship with your ex-spouse. Why? Because you love your children. And that love, my friend, will be the driving motivation that will push you to do some of the things I am about to talk about.

The key to making use of *The Parental Peace Accord* successful is a harmonious working relationship between the divorced parents. Of course, right now you're saying, "Bailey, you're an idiot! If we could have had a harmonious working relationship we wouldn't have gotten divorced!" Well, I would like to make a distinction here. Perhaps you couldn't have a harmonious working relationship as *spouses*, but that doesn't preclude you from having a harmonious working relationship as *parenting partners*! After all, you have an incredible common bond which will serve as a foundation for such a relationship: the deep love you both have for your children.

So where do you start? How do you go about being proactive in making the peace accord between you and your ex-spouse a harmonious working relationship? Well, there is a secret method to make this happen. I can only hope that you are ready for it. This method is the result of years and years of trial and error. It is so profound that many divorced couples have found that the difficulty in utilizing this method is far overshadowed by the tremendous results. Are you ready? I won't make you wait any longer. I won't keep you in suspense anymore. Here it is: *do the right thing*.

Oh, you smirk. You scoff at such a build up for such a simple and short statement. Doubt if you must, but I will tell you that if more divorced parents simply did the right thing when it came to dealing with each other, not only would their lives be less stressful, but also more importantly, their children would be grateful benefactors. If you want to be proactive about building a harmonious working relationship with your children's other parent, I would encourage you to go out of your way to do the right thing, regardless of whether or not your ex-spouse is. It's that "high road" attitude that will always serve you well, especially when it comes to your children.

Here's an easy example. You have young children. They have no source of income other than maybe a small allowance, and they have no real mode of transportation. So along comes Christmas or a birthday. Now you may not really expect anything from your children on Christmas or on your birthday because of their limited or nonexistent income and a lack of transportation, but the fact is, that does not mean they don't want to get you something—even if it is just a card. And the fact is, they feel the same way about your ex-spouse.

So, I suggest you do the right thing. Give them some money so that they can buy their other parent a small gift, or at least a card. Offer to take them to the store so they can get it. Don't take them along with you when you go to the store; make it a special trip. Heck, make it an outing and stop to get something to eat. The benefits of this small gesture are greater than you can imagine.

First of all, your children are going to remember how you helped them do something they couldn't do for themselves. And believe it or not, that little bit of time you spent sitting across from them eating ice cream left a lasting memory on their young minds. Your children are also going to subconsciously realize that you are a good person for doing such a thing when it seemed there would be no apparent benefit in it for you.

Secondly, your ex-spouse is no idiot. He or she knows that the children don't have the resources or the mobility to do such a thing on their own without some assistance from you. This small act of kindness sends a message to your parenting partner that you respect him or her as your children's other parent. It also tells your ex-spouse that you take a positive approach with your children where your ex-spouse is concerned. In short, this small, proactive gesture creates a lot of goodwill in fostering a commitment from both of you to the principles of *The Parental Peace Accord*.

Of course, some of you will feel that this is a one-way deal because your ex-spouse would never go out of his or her way to do this type of thing for you. Maybe. But this is a win-win situation for you. If both parents are engaging in this kind of conduct, then everybody will benefit from the positive environment that is created. If you are doing this type of thing and your ex-spouse isn't, your children will grow up recognizing the person who took the high road in life and set a good example for them.

Be Accommodating

Another way of doing the right thing is by doing what you can to accommodate your parenting partner when it comes to your children's events and activities. It's unfortunate that so many single custodial parents find themselves in a scheduling bind because they can't get off work in time to get their children to practices or to medical appointments. Too many times the attitude of the non-custodial parent is that it is the custodial parent's responsibility. While this may be true, that doesn't prevent the non-custodial parent from being a supportive parenting partner.

This approach of accommodating the other parent isn't that much different from what I discussed in Chapter Seven regarding visitation. In that chapter I suggested that the non-custodial parent ask the custodial parent for the first right to see the children when there was a need for a baby-sitter. I would encourage that same spirit of cooperation when it comes to scheduling accommodations. The non-custodial parent should make the offer for the custodial parent to contact them when there is a scheduling conflict or logistics challenge.

Again, doing the right thing creates a win-win situation for everyone. It makes for a positive environment for the parents in their attempt to work within the principles of *The Parental Peace Accord*. It also helps the children and reinforces their knowledge and security that *both* of their parents are there for them. Lastly, it helps the custodial parenting partners to face the challenging circumstances of being single parents.

Another thing the courts encourage, but have a difficult time enforcing, is communication. Certainly, good communication between divorced parents is imperative for *The Parental Peace Accord* to even have a chance of being successful. But this is an area where you can take a proactive approach by doing the right thing.

Tell the non-custodial parent how the dentist appointment went. Make a copy of the school report card so that they are in the loop with regard to your child's education. Let your parenting partner know about upcoming parent-teacher conferences. I can tell you that based on our interactions at parent-teacher conferences, the vast majority of my sons' teachers had no clue their mother and I were divorced.

Here's another important area of communication. Let your parenting partner know of the children's accomplishments. It is important for your children to receive positive reinforcement when they do the right thing. Your ex-spouse should be a part of this. In all likelihood, your children will not go bragging about themselves to the other parent. I remember one time, when I was standing in line at the grocery store, a woman behind me asked if I was Ross' father. I replied that I was, and she went on to tell me that she was one of his high school teachers and what a joy he was to have as a student. It's times like that when you feel all the effort of working with your ex-spouse is well worth it. I shared that with my ex-wife because she deserved to have those feelings of pride and accomplishment as well.

Okay, so you say that you and your ex-spouse aren't really at the point when it is that easy to pick up the phone and do all this communicating stuff. This is not uncommon. This whole concept of two divorced parents having a peace accord for the benefit of their children is an ongoing, evolutionary process. So, as the therapists always like to say, "Take baby steps."

Perhaps a good way to begin this communication process is with an e-mail. It's pretty easy and non-threatening. I suggest starting out your e-mail with "Just thought I would drop you a note to let you know that..." Maybe you won't get a response—at least not initially—but that's not the point. The point is you are taking a proactive approach by doing the right thing and communicating with to your child's other parent.

If your ex-spouse doesn't have e-mail, start out with phone messages, faxes, or regular mail. As a last resort you could send sealed envelopes with your children, but I really don't like this because it can make your children feel as though they're caught in the middle or that they're acting as your carrier pigeon. The important thing is to find a good way to communicate. If you do this, no matter how difficult it may seem, it will only get easier and lead to more open communication.

Many people who have taken me up on the suggestion to be proactive and use friendly e-mail correspondence to keep the other parent advised of what's going on with the children have reported that those e-mails eventually led to pretty comfortable verbal communication with their ex-spouses. If you remember why you're doing it, it makes it a lot easier. You're doing it for the benefit of your children. My sons knew their mother and I were communicating fairly frequently and openly—not because they witnessed it, but because that was the only way Mom and Dad could both know what they knew!

Now, for some of you, what I am about to suggest will really seem like pushing the envelope. In time, as the divorce wounds heal, take it upon yourself to do a favor for your ex-spouse when he or she needs it. (I know, I can hear it now.) "Look, Bailey, I don't mind doing some of this stuff for the benefit my kids, but I'm not in it to help out my ex with things that have nothing to do with my kids."

Maybe not, but is it really going to kill you to show her where the reset button is on the garbage disposal? And is it going to alter your life to explain to him the difference between baking soda and baking powder? Come on, after all, your kids use the garbage disposal too. And you certainly don't want them eating something that will seal their jaws shut. More importantly, it is this additional proactive conduct that creates a cooperative spirit of doing the right thing.

I'm not saying that doing the right thing is always going to be the easiest way or the path of least resistance. It really requires parents to allow some of the traditional rules of dissolution to get a little fuzzy. You can't always get locked in on a "my time vs. your time" mentality. Plus, it would be counterproductive to the process of *The Parental Peace Accord* for you to have a rigid interpretation of your responsibilities and your ex-spouse's responsibilities.

Color Outside The Lines

When I was a kid I was always told by my grade-school teachers to stay in the lines when coloring. Boy, if you ever wanted to mess with those teachers' minds, all you had to do was just ask them why you had to stay inside the lines. They would get that befuddled look and say "Because you're supposed to!" You're supposed to? What does *that* mean?

It means go with the flow. Follow the court's orders. Remember, divorced parents aren't supposed to get along. Just do it like everybody else. You're divorced now, so let your ex-spouse fend for himself or herself like everybody else does. Do what is expected. People expect you to have nothing good to say about your ex-spouse, regardless of the fact that your ex-spouse is your children's parent. Stay inside the lines.

Fortunately, today's teachers are more inclined to teach our children that it is okay to color outside of the lines. They understand that by permitting this, they are allowing the children to express themselves and push new boundaries. I'm suggesting the same thing for divorced adults. It's okay to color outside of the lines. It's okay to have a working relationship with your ex-spouse. You're allowed to be there and support each other as parenting partners. And yes, you're even permitted to like each other if it finally comes to that. Go ahead, color outside the lines for your children. They deserve it.

If there is no way on earth that the two of you will ever get along and work together for the benefit of your children, then you should stay inside the lines when you color and follow the court's orders to the letter. But if you are both committed to the principles outlined in this book, be willing to color outside the lines and willing to put out the extra effort to do the right thing. In addition, be willing to allow your parenting partner to color outside the lines.

Now again, just so you don't think I live in la-la land, I understand that there are some ex-spouses who will never get it. I understand that some of them are monsters. And I understand that these ex-spouses will never be true parenting partners, and they will never do the right thing. I have represented parents with these ex-spouses, and I have represented those ex-spouses. For every horror story you can tell me, I can probably one up you with one I have heard in my law office. So what do you do?

You do the right thing. That's right. Even if your ex-spouse won't do the right thing, and even if your ex-spouse is a monster, do the right thing. If you're in this situation, your path will be a little harder and a lot more frustrating. But you still must do the right thing. You've all heard the old lesson, "two wrongs don't make a right." The same is true as applied to *The Parental Peace Accord*.

It is tempting to ignore and/or avoid an ex-spouse who is resentful, mean, addicted or just plain uncaring. But good or bad, that person is still the other parent of your children, and there is a very good chance that your children has feelings for them. Lashing out at your ex or trying to get even only escalates the negativity between the two of you and provides not one benefit for your children.

Many times I have seen divorced parents allow their lives to be consumed with a hatred for their ex-spouses. These parents will go to great lengths to make the others' lives miserable. They live for it. They expend great effort in figuring out ways to aggravate each other. They will continually play games just to frustrate the other parent.

I recall a father who would never pay his child's medical bills and who was always late with child support. Eventually, the mother would file for contempt proceedings, at which time all the payments due would be immediately paid. I also knew a mother who wouldn't give her ex-spouse the children's medical bills to pay because she knew that eventually the health-care providers would turn them over to collection agencies and that in time, her ex-husband's credit would be ruined.

Of course, this was no worse than the parent who would specifically not tell their ex-spouse about their children's extracurricular activities just so they wouldn't have to see the other parent. And then they could point out to their children that the other parent didn't show up. You don't have to be a genius to figure out who loses when parents, fueled by uncontrolled hatred, play these silly games.

Sometimes this type of behavior by parents can have unexpected consequences. I knew a child who appeared to have a great relationship with both of his parents. Nevertheless, he would always ask his parents not to tell the other one about his extra-curricular activities. It didn't make sense. If Dad knew about the tryouts, the boy would ask him not to tell his mother. If Mom knew about the game, he would ask her not to tell his father. But there was no question the boy had a great relationship with both parents.

Finally, the child's motive was revealed. His parents hated each other so much and their behavior toward each other was so obnoxious that the son was embarrassed by them. In fact, even if the parents did not engage in embarrassing behavior, their moods became so foul at the sight of each other that it would ruin the rest of the evening for the son. Since the parents were not smart enough to figure out the negative effects their emotions were having on their son, the boy took it upon himself to solve the problem by requesting that one parent not tell the other one about his activities.

This kind of hatred and negative feelings are emotionally draining and counterproductive to the principles of *The Parental Peace Accord.* More importantly, a parent should be ashamed for creating such an environment for children who were not part of the divorce decision-making process. Again, children deserve happy childhood memories. This is only going to happen in a divorce environment if parents are committed to doing the right thing. Of course I'm going to say it. It's about the kids, not you.

Notes and Thoughts

_____

_____

_____

_____

_____

_____

_____

_____

_____

_____

_____

_____

_____

_____

_____

12 | EXPECTATIONS

There is a psychological theory that holds that all emotions, both positive and negative, are the result of met and unmet expectations. When you walk into your house after work, your expectation is that things will be just as you left them that morning. When you open the door and find the living room has been decorated for your surprise birthday party, and you are greeted by friends and family, your expectation was not met, and a positive emotion was created.

Conversely, unmet expectations may more often than not create negative emotions. I remember once when I came home from work and all three of our emptied trash cans and their lids were lying across the yard where the trash collectors had thrown them. My teenage son had been home from school for hours, and I was quite put out that he had not had the common courtesy to pick them up and return them to the garage. After all, he had to walk right by them when he got home from school!

Okay, this is a fairly typical experience for anybody enduring life with teenage kids. But what was really going on? Quite simply, I had the expectation that my honor roll student, being the responsible person he was, would certainly pick up the trash cans and their lids when he had to walk by them to get into the house. That expectation was not met, and a negative emotion was created. All of this is quite natural and very normal. However, in the grand scheme of things, would it really make a difference in my life or his if he did not take the trash cans into the garage? Of course not.

Obviously, you can have positive emotions when expectations are met. If we expect our children to make good grades and they do, we're pleased. If we expect a year-end bonus from our employer and we get it, we're pleased. The point is, expectations have a tremendous impact on our emotions. This is doubly true for our children.

When I was in college, I was intrigued by a theory that was being promoted by my child psychology professor. He stated that, deep in their hearts, children actually desire discipline, although they would rarely recognize or even acknowledge this. However, discipline gives them a foundation and structure which provide a stable environment. They know what is expected of them and what to expect of their parents. In short, the expectations are clearly defined.

Additionally, this structure and discipline, when administered properly, have a unique way of letting your children know you love them. Any time that my children were grounded or punished in some form, I always reminded them in a very calm, matter-of-fact way that *because* I loved them, I had an obligation to punish them for their misbehavior. I would inquire of them as to what kind of father would I be—and what message would I be sending—if I were to just ignore their wrong deeds and express no concern. In all likelihood, they would probably feel as though I really didn't care, and that is not a loving message. My sons, like most children, have questioned me on several things in their lives, but I doubt they ever questioned my love for them.

If you and your spouse have maintained and practiced certain rules and discipline with your children, it is extremely important that you continue to do so after the marriage has dissolved. This keeps the expectations consistent for your children and subconsciously gives them some of the stability and structure they will need.

After I was divorced, I recall a time when my oldest son, who was about seven or eight at the time, made some very disrespectful remarks to his mother. She communicated this to me, and I took it upon myself to discuss it with him and issue some form of punishment. The incident sent some very strong and positive messages. First and foremost, it made it clear to him that type of conduct would not be tolerated by either of his parents. Secondly, Mom and Dad were still united as to what was right and wrong behavior. In other words, Mom and Dad were divorced, but they were still Mom and Dad, and their expectations had not changed.

Just as important, parents must realize that their children have certain expectations of them which won't change just because Mom and Dad went separate ways in their lives. For instance, if your little girl has a dance recital, she expects both Mom and Dad to be there. In fact, it is imperative that both parents be there to reassure her that, divorce or no divorce, Mom and Dad will *always* be there for her.

I have had a number of clients who would make out schedules as to which one was going to attend which event. All of this was designed so they wouldn't have to see each other. My advice is quite simple: Get over it! You can bet that the game you don't go to will be the one in which your son hits a home run and you weren't there to share it with him. Imagine hearing him say, "Gosh, I can't believe you didn't get to see it!"

"But Mr. Bailey, what if my ex brings a date?. I just can't take that." Okay, let's get our priorities straight. Yes, you may experience some emotional pangs from seeing your ex with another person enjoying the extraordinary performance of your child. But who is this about anyway, you or your child? If this type of situation is getting in the way of allowing your child to have both parents present for his or her life experiences, then it is important to consider counseling and to focus on what is best for your child.

The situation will not go away, and if it isn't an issue now, it may be in the future. You and your former spouse have a life of parent-child experiences ahead. There is a strong possibility that your ex-spouse will have someone else in his or her life. But the fact is that your children will have dances, games, weddings, and grandchildren. And guess what? They have a valid expectation that you both will be there for those things. Once again, the marriage may have ended, but the parenting responsibilities go on forever.

Inadvertent Expectations

As long as we are talking about expectations, you should watch out for ones you might inadvertently create. I'll give you an example. My wife and I divorced when our sons were seven and three. We tried to do all the right things for our children. We worked hard to have good communication, we both attended their games, and we were united on the discipline front. In fact, we were getting along so well that we took the boys out for pizza together so they would know that even though Mom and Dad were divorced, they were responsible adults who were cordial to each other and loved their children very much.

Storybook ending, right? Wrong! The evening went so well that our three-year-old told the seven-year-old, "I think Mom and Dad are going to get back together because you can tell they still like each other." Imagine our shock and how we both wanted to run to tell our son that there was no way in hell that was going to happen! Instead we explained to him that yes, we were friends; yes, we both loved him and his brother very much; but no, Mommy and Daddy were not getting together again. Suffice it to say the four of us didn't have dinner together again until the kids were little older and we had moved on with our lives.

When discussing how parents can inadvertently create expectations, remember the old adage, "Say what you mean and mean what you say." If you tell your child you're going to do something, do it! It is unbelievable how many different ways parents can create false expectations for their children. Picture the child on the team who is desperately trying to locate his parent in the stands because that parent promised to be there, or the little girl who has her clothes packed for a weekend visitation and is waiting expectantly for a parent who doesn't show.

If parents knew the adverse effects these unmet expectations have on their children, they would be stunned. The emotional impacts can be as diverse as disappointment, sadness, anger, or just feeling the parent doesn't really care. The only way to avoid this is through good communication and doing what you say you will do. Yes, things come up and there are emergencies, but at least call or contact your child and let him or her know why you can't do what you said you would, how disappointed you are, and how much you wanted to be there. Your children want to believe you care, and all you have to do is make a little effort to show them.

This expectation business is really pretty serious stuff. Begin with the fact that your children had the natural expectation that Mom and Dad would always be married. Okay, that didn't happen. Think about how that unmet expectation was dealt with. Was it even discussed? It is amazing how many parents start the entire divorce process without ever having had an in-depth, sincere discussion about it with their children. As I discussed in Chapter Three, the manner in which this news is delivered and handled is critical.

It is also important to remember that depending on their age, children have different expectations. Toddlers and adolescents are subconsciously focused more on love, security, and stability—basically knowing that Mom and Dad will be there for them. Teenagers and adult children are more inclined to be focused on the expectation that even though Mom and Dad have gotten divorced, they won't put them in the middle of it. In other words, the parent-child relationships will remain the same, and the children won't have to take sides during the divorce or its aftermath.

Whatever the age, it is imperative that you step back from your own emotions and consider the expectations that your child may have. If they are not being met, how is that impacting the child, and what is being done about it?

When I was in the third grade, I lived in California and the person whom I considered my father would pick me up every day after school. When I arrived at home, I would have an after-school snack and then go outside to play—a pretty typical life for a third-grader. One day, I wasn't picked up after school. The man whom I had assumed was my father had been arrested for white-collar crimes and I was picked up by a couple of government agents who were waiting for me at the principal's office. I wasn't taken home, but instead ended up at the state welfare department and was placed in an orphanage. Imagine how many expectations were unmet in only a single day!

But in retrospect, I realize there was another issue of equal importance. While everybody and everything was done to make sure this third-grader had food, shelter, and clothing, nobody ever addressed the emotional turmoil he felt from so many of his childhood expectations being unmet. To keep everything in perspective, we can offer the weak excuse that the people involved were government workers, not parents. But *you* are a parent, and you have a responsibility to consider the natural expectations your children have and how your divorce will impact those expectations.

There are also expectations that children have that were developed during your marriage. I'll give you a great example. In family law circles there is a great constitutional/jurisdictional argument regarding college education. Generally speaking, there isn't a court in the country that can force *married* parents to pay for their children's college educations. It is not uncommon for many families to never have, nor expect, their children to go to college. It is also true that there are many parents who can't afford to send their children to college, and if they were to go, it would only be through scholarships, grants, and student loans.

However, those same courts now have the authority to mandate divorcing or divorced parents to pay for their children's college educations as a form of child support when considering the best interest of the children. How does that come about? Quite often the objective of the court is going to be to provide the child with the same standard of living that might have existed had the divorce not occurred. In other words, based on the standard of living at the time of the divorce, the court may reasonably assume that if the parents had not gotten a divorce they would have sent their children to college.

So what are we really saying? We're saying that domestic family law actually considers the reasonable expectation children might have about receiving a college education; notwithstanding the fact their parents are getting a divorce. As an example, where there are two college-educated, financially successful parents, the court may find it reasonable to order those parents to provide college educations for their children. Based on their standard of living at the time of the divorce, it would be reasonable to expect that they would send their children to college had they not gotten divorced. Conversely, and again as an example, where there are two uneducated parents living in a lower income bracket, the court may refrain from making a college education order because their standard of living at the time of the divorce would not have created the expectation that the parents would send their children to college.

Although these are generalities and opposite examples, I think you can get the point I am making about how expectations play into the dissolution process. Hopefully you can see that your children have emotional, financial, and physical expectations, just to name a few. Your job is to identify those expectations and determine if they are being met. If you sense they are not being met, then you have no choice but to address those expectations, even if it may be painful or uncomfortable.

Expectation Difficulties

As I mentioned above, with younger children it is not too difficult to figure out their expectations. They expect Mom and Dad to always be there for them. They subconsciously expect to live in a stable and secure environment. Most importantly, they expect to feel loved. However, I've had many parents tell me they have no clue what their older children expect. These parents express frustration with what was once a typical parent-teenager communication challenge before the divorce, but has now become even more stressed and strained after the divorce.

Here's something you might consider trying with older children, even adult children. A few years ago, I was participating in an executive coaching program called The Strategic Coach®, which was founded by Dan Sullivan. During one particular session, an exercise was introduced which was referred to as The R-Factor Question®. In effect, the R-Factor Question® was "If we were sitting here one year from today, what would have to happen for you to feel good about your success?" For executives, this is a powerful question and one that can lead to some incredible strategic planning because you can insert any time frame you desire.

I suggest that in the proper context, the same approach could be used to determine the expectations of older children. When the time and mood is right, I think there could be some potential success in a dialogue such as the following:

"I know that this divorce throws our family into some emotional challenges, to say the least. It's just important to me that you know how much I really love you and that I want you to be happy. I can't change the divorce, but I am here for you, and I want to do what is right. Let me ask you something. If we were sitting here a year from now, what would have to happen for you to feel good about our progress in getting through this?"

The Strategic Coach's R-Factor Question® placed within the context of that kind of honest dialogue might very well give you some surprising insights into the expectations of your child. Additionally, as Dan Sullivan might say, you could realize some great "strategic by-products." An honest conversation with your child may open up a new level of communication between the two of you. It may also send a strong message to your child that you really do care and you really do think about how all of this is affecting him or her.

Now understand that this approach with a teenager may not be as easy as it sounds. There is a very good chance that when you ask that question you will get that stock teenage mumble, "I don't know." My advice? Don't push, but certainly persevere with some in-context, open-ended questions such as, "Well, what is it that worries you the most about our divorce?" or "Tell me, what is the biggest effect this divorce is having on you?" If the tenor of the discussion is one of quiet, genuine concern, as opposed to relentless needling, there is a pretty good chance your child will eventually respond to these types of questions, and then you can return to the r-factor question in an effort to identify expectations.

For *The Parental Peace Accord* to work for you, your ex-spouse, and your children, it is just as important to remember that you and your ex-spouse are entitled to have certain expectations of each other as well. First and foremost, you should both be able to reasonably expect the other to act in good faith when it comes to addressing issues of the dissolution. You should feel comfortable that the other isn't doing or saying anything with a hidden agenda or ulterior motive. There is nothing that will undermine the efforts of your accord more than a distrust of the other party.

I'm not naïve. I certainly understand that many divorces come about as a result of trust being violated, and those are the people who will think I'm crazy to suggest or even think that their ex spouses could ever be trusted. If that's the case, then discuss it. You owe it to your children. Lay it all out on the table. Tell your ex-spouse that you don't know whether you will ever be able to trust him or her again, but that for the sake of the children and to make your parental peace accord work, you are willing to give him or her another chance with your trust. I know. Just suck it up, and remember you are doing this for your children, not your ex-spouse.

Along this same line, you and your ex-spouse should be able to expect the other to refrain from bad-mouthing or sabotaging the other's relationships with the children. As I discussed in Chapter Four, there are no winners when parents degrade or speak ill of their children's other parent. This kind of personal venting may give you some momentary satisfaction or feelings of fulfillment, but you would be doing an enormous disservice to your children.

It is also reasonable for one parent to expect the other to support them in their parenting. Excluding some awful parenting behavior or something potentially harmful to the children, parents operating under *The Parental Peace Accord* should give the other parent the benefit of the doubt that their ex-spouse is doing what they truly feel is in the best interest of the children. Yes, there will be times when you will disagree. But there is a difference between disagreeing with each other and undermining the parental relationships between your ex-spouse and your children. Again, unless there is some awful behavior or something potentially harmful to your children, you should support each other's parenting decisions, even if you would have handled the situation a little differently.

So, there it is. Children have expectations of their parents. Divorced parents have expectations of each other. If those expectations are not identified, addressed, and met, there is sure to be some emotional unrest. It won't always be easy to explore these expectations, especially those of your ex-spouse. But let your motivation be that your children deserve it. They deserve to have their reasonable expectations identified and met. And they deserve for you and your ex-spouse to know each other's expectations. Realize that this is an effort undertaken to avoid conflicts and to promote the goals of your peace accord, which two of you have made for the benefit of your children.

I should make one final note on this topic. This business of identifying, addressing, and meeting expectations will always be a work in progress. In other words, in all probability, the expectations that you and your ex-spouse have, as well as those of your children, will change as the children mature and circumstances of the family environment change. So be tolerant and flexible. After all, it's not about you…it's about the children.

Notes and Thoughts

_____

_____

_____

_____

_____

_____

_____

_____

_____

_____

_____

13 | THERE'S A STRANGER IN THE HOUSE

Yes, there is life after divorce. It just takes some longer than others to find it. Everyone will have different hurts, wounds, and insecurities. Everyone will have different rates of healing. Even a person who has gone through a relatively uncomplicated divorce will still be a little apprehensive about getting emotionally involved with someone new. It's just an instinctive defense mechanism. Nobody wants to put themselves in the position to get hurt again.

No, you're not the first person to say, "I will *never* get married again." In fact, I wish I had a dollar for every time I heard a client say that—only to remarry at a later date. The fact is we can't help ourselves. We belong to a species that prefers companionship. For some, this preference will manifest itself in the form of a girlfriend or boyfriend. For others, it will result in remarriage. And others will stand by their declaration to never marry again by choosing instead to live with their "significant other."

I'm not sure there is any right or wrong answer here. I think every person has to do what is right for them and what is right for their children. Of course, there are religious issues linked to every aspect of this subject, but I'm not even going to go near that debate. The bottom line is that it is perfectly natural, and it is reasonable to expect that someone will come along whom you are attracted to and want to see more often. When that happens, it is only a matter of time before this person is introduced to your children. The secret to accomplishing this and still having harmony in your life lies in the approach.

There are a zillion issues, aspects, and ramifications that come into play when you bring another person into your life, or more importantly, into the lives of your children. In recognition that you probably have a lot going on right now, I promised to keep this book short. Therefore, I won't discuss all one zillion of these things, but I do want to hit on the more important ones. There are many variables to consider, such as: your children's ages, the length of time since your divorce, the personalities of your children, the personality of the new person in your life, and the extent of that new relationship. I'll try to give all of these and a few others adequate discussion.

The first factor to consider is how your children will meet this new person in your life. Is this a person who they know through school or church? Is it a person who they introduced to you? Is it a person who they first met when he came to the house to pick you up for a dinner date? Or maybe it's not a new person at all, but somebody whom you and the children have known for a long time.

Delicate Introductions

In any event, there is a pretty good chance that when this person becomes someone you are dating, there will be some delicate introductions involved. It is very possible that your children will be apprehensive or downright resentful toward this new person. Before you become overwhelmed with feelings of frustration, guilt, or unfairness, put yourself in your children's perspective for a moment.

Your children have probably only known you to love or show signs of affection toward one other person in their life, their other parent. This is the same other parent who they probably still love and care about. It is quite reasonable for them to feel a little confused when they see your affections directed to this new person. Depending on your children's ages, their feelings, which they may be unable to identify, might manifest themselves in the form of various behaviors.

If careful groundwork hasn't been laid, the younger children are going to experience the most confusion. They don't have, nor can they be expected to have, the emotional maturity to understand why Mommy or Daddy would want to see someone else when they could just as easily see one another. They won't understand how this person could come in and take Mommy or Daddy's time and attention away from them. To them, this stranger is intruding on their way of life.

Older children may have exactly the same kind of feelings, but these feelings might manifest themselves in a completely different way. Rather than confusion, they may exhibit resentment toward this new relationship. They may still feel a loyalty to their other parent, and the last thing they will want is *another* parent. This resentment may show itself in the form of coldness, rudeness, or even sabotage. We've all seen those comedic movies in which the children plot to make sure Mom's new relationship doesn't happen. The problem is that in real life, it is not always that funny.

Another factor to be considered is the length of time that has passed since the divorce. First of all, don't expect me to give you a time that is appropriate. There just isn't any right answer to that one. It depends on the children, their ages, the circumstances surrounding the divorce, how long the divorce took to complete, and a myriad of other dynamics. Obviously, if you're bringing a new person home a few weeks after the divorce, it's probably reasonable to assume that neither you nor your children have had an adequate amount of time to adjust. You're probably headed toward a rebound relationship and your kids are probably wondering if you've lost your mind.

As long as we're on this delicate subject, let me explore another area with you. If your divorce was the result of you seeing someone else outside of the marriage, I wouldn't hold my breath waiting for your children to accept this person. You may have been smitten with this person during your extramarital affair, but there is a pretty good chance your children will see this person as a home-wrecker and their resentment levels will be high. Not only are you seeing someone else, but you're seeing the person who caused you and your children's other parent to get divorced. In all likelihood, their initial feelings are not going to be warm and fuzzy.

If you find yourself in this circumstance, just remember this: you created the situation, not your children. You had the extramarital affair, not your children. The worst thing you can do is to respond to your children's normal feelings of resentment in this situation with your own resentment toward them for not accepting your paramour. I'm not sitting in judgment on this issue; I'm just forcing you to face the reality of a child's normal reaction. If you've made this bed (no pun intended), the only way you'll be able to sleep in it (okay, maybe intended) is to have some very long, honest, heartfelt conversations with your children. Even with that, success may hinge on the ages and levels of emotional understanding of your children.

I can hear you now. You're saying, "Hell, Bailey, if I listen to you, I may as well go jump off a bridge because I am obviously never going to have another relationship as long as I care about and consider my children!" I would suggest you stay off the bridge.

It is very possible and plausible for you to have a relationship and live happily ever after. If you will recall, I made an earlier reference to careful groundwork. When I speak of careful groundwork, I am not referring to tricking your children or setting them up. I am referring to taking their perspectives into consideration and handling things in such a way that when you move on in your life, you do it in such a way that they can accept it. Remember the cornerstone principle of *The Parental Peace Accord*. It's about the children, not you.

Certainly, the most effective approach is honesty. Being honest is a way to involve your children in the process, and it doesn't give them surprise situations to deal with. Assuming your children are no longer toddlers, why not be honest with them and say, "There's this guy at work who asked me out to dinner. I'm not sure what to do. What do you think"?

First, this kind of approach will send your children the immediate message that they are more important to you than the guy at work. Second, it is good for your children's self-esteem to learn that you value their counsel in such personal matters. Additionally, they might ask you some questions that you should consider, such as, "Do you want to go out with him?" "What's he like?" and "How did you meet him?" Last, and most importantly, it makes them part of the process. They most likely will say something like, "You should go out with him. What have you got to lose?" Afterwards they will probably want to know how it went and get a reading on your feelings toward this person. Take it slow; you're giving your kids a lot to digest emotionally.

If your kids are very young, this dating thing has a different set of rules. Because your children are young, they need you more and will not want to share you with anyone else. On the other hand, because they are younger, they will not be able to read as much into things, and therefore, may be a little more flexible.

Another thing to consider if your children are young is baby-sitting. I wouldn't suggest that the first time you leave your children with a baby-sitter is also the first time they know you're going out on a date. The association is just too strong for youngsters to overcome. In the beginning, I encourage you to use a baby-sitter for less threatening things, such as a parent-teacher meeting, a night out with the guys/girls, or a doctor's appointment. When your children realize that sometimes Mommy or Daddy has to be away and somebody has to watch them, then it's not a new routine when or if you enter the dating waters.

First Impressions

There's an old saying that advises, "You only get to make a first impression once." This is advice you and anybody you date should remember. Children are extremely impressionable. How they cope with the idea of your seeing someone else, how they meet that person, and the circumstances and groundwork laid prior to that meeting will have a great influence in determining your child's acceptance of the situation.

Kids aren't stupid. They're pretty hard to fool. Most of the time they see right through us adults. The best advice you can give your new friend is to just be honest and be yourself. If this new person comes in all rah-rah and gushy, trying to impress your children, they will probably think this person is a flake. If your date comes in quiet and detached so as to not intimidate your children, they will probably think this new person has the personality of a doorknob. Or if the person you introduce your children to seems too good to be true, your children may think he or she is a manipulative gold-digger or someone trying to take advantage of the situation. In any of these cases, never underestimate the fact that your children might be right!

Another aspect of this topic is the type of relationship involved and how far it has evolved. Is it just a harmless first-time dinner date, or is this someone you have been dating for a year? Has the relationship evolved to the point that this person is going to move and "live-in" your home, or is there a marriage in the future? These questions get back to our discussion in Chapter Twelve about expectations, or more importantly, unmet expectations.

Once again, the best way to avoid unmet expectations is through open and honest dialogue with you children. If this is a first-time, low-key date, let them know so their imaginations aren't running wild. If they know you've been seeing someone for an extended period of time and you find yourself becoming closer to this person, keep your kids in the loop so that they aren't caught off guard later.

This doesn't mean that you need to give your children a blow-by-blow of every detail of the relationship. It just means be open with them and let them know through your honesty where you are in the relationship. If you are honest with them, they will probably be just as honest with you. Sometimes this can be good and sometimes this can be bad.

It's great if they tell you they really like the person and that they're glad you're happy. It's not so great if they tell you that they think the person you're seeing is a loser and you just don't see it. In that case, it doesn't necessarily mean your children are right, as their opinions may be skewed by other factors. It's possible that they are still working through some dissolution issues. It is also possible that things are moving too fast for them. Another possibility is that they might just be right! I always encourage parents to have an open mind regarding their children's opinions about who they are seeing and to ask themselves if it is possible that their children are right. Like I said, kids are pretty smart, and it's pretty tough to get something by them.

Another common situation is when a divorced person decides to live with someone he or she is seeing. Again, I won't even go near the moral debates on this issue. The fact is that it happens all the time, and this book is designed to assist parents in following *The Parental Peace Accord* process for the benefit of their children. This brings us to the first question to consider about living with a new love interest. Is it best for the children? Ouch! Tough question, isn't it?

Well, it is certainly in the children's best interest for their parents to be happy, provided that happiness doesn't cause unhappiness for the children. So is living with someone who makes you very happy the best thing for your children? To answer this, the best place to go is to the children themselves. Here's a new concept: Ask them. If this person has been really good to them and made you happy, they may not only approve but may be excited at the prospect. If this is the case, you're probably doing the right thing.

If your children are still living at home, still your responsibility, and don't want to live with this other person, then the answer is simple. No. If that wasn't the answer you wanted to hear, too bad. If you think I'm being too harsh and abrupt, you're wrong. And you know why, don't you? Because it's not about you, it's about the children. As I said in the introduction of this book, not all decisions are going to be easy or fun, but once you accept the concept that the children come first, then the answers become very obvious.

Remarriage

Okay, when you got divorced you said you would never get married again, but now you're actually considering it. Of course you are. It's perfectly natural to fall in love again and find someone you want to share life with. I am pleased to tell you that your contemplated nuptials are allowable under *The Parental Peace Accord*—with one condition. Oh, come on, you knew I was going to say it. Your new marriage is the right thing to do provided it is in the best interest of your children.

Again, the first and best thing to do is ask them. Tell your children how you feel, but also tell them you want to know how they feel. It's interesting that there used to be a tradition requiring a man to ask a woman's father for permission to marry her. What if we required the same thing of divorced parents, but the intended had to ask the children? "What?" you say, "What if the children said 'no'?" Well, I don't know. What if the father said no? I'm sure many fathers refused, and while many couples abided by that wish, many did not.

The point is to put the children first and to do what is in their best interest. I know many people will think I am crazy to suggest this approach. They claim that I have gone too far and am now putting the children in control of their parents' lives. They are missing the point. What I am really saying is to consider your children's feelings and opinions on things that have a direct impact on their lives.

There is no question that there are times when it would be in the best interest of the children for their parents to remarry, but they, the children, may not see it. There is no question that some children are too young to even understand the concept of divorce and marriage, much less to know what is best for them. The point is to ask yourself what impact your remarriage would have on your children. By determining whether that impact would be positive or negative and then by acting accordingly, you have put the children first and done what is in their best interest.

Now, I've spent a lot of time discussing approaches for parents who find themselves interested in seeing someone new. In terms of *The Parental Peace Accord,* the other side of this equation is the approach for the parents who are watching their ex-spouses move on with their lives. Again, there are a lot of factors that could make this process easier or even more difficult.

If the parents have been divorced for a number of years, it is usually easier and more palatable for one to see the other moving on than if it had only been a few weeks since the dissolution. Similarly, if *you* are involved with someone else, it makes it easier to see your ex-spouse also become involved. Easy stuff, right?

But what if you're still in love with your ex-spouse? What if you're not involved with someone else and fear nobody will ever take an interest in you again? What if you're afraid your children will like this new person more than you? What if you don't think this new person is the right person for your ex-spouse? Ah, dealing with all of those "what-ifs" isn't quite as easy.

The principle idea here is that none of the things mentioned in the previous two paragraphs are the central issue. When considering your ex-spouse's involvement with another person, your challenge is to determine which response on your part would be in the best interest of your children. Is it really going to serve your children well for you to exhibit anger, jealousy, or smugness?

Your objective is to be supportive of your children and help them feel secure and stable in the environment in which they live. And in case you forgot, you are one-half of the duo that put them in this environment. That can't be changed. But what you can do is be there for them and help them as the different scenarios unfold before them.

"Did you hear Mom is seeing this guy?"

"Yeah, how do you feel about that?"

"Well, he seems nice, and he makes Mom pretty happy."

"Well, your Mom deserves to be happy as long as he's good to her and you kids."

Nobody said this was going to be easy. As tough as it may be, you have to set aside your personal feelings and make sure your children know that you are always there for them and that they can come to you any time they want to talk about *their* feelings. When they do come to you to talk, make sure you listen. Also, make sure the children are being honest about their feelings. They might feel the need to say what they think you want to hear.

"Dad, this guy knows nothing about sports!"

"Mom, this woman doesn't hold a candle to you in the kitchen. I don't think she even knows how to boil water!"

These kinds of statements are easy traps to fall into. There's nothing more fun than getting together with the kids and ganging up on the new person. The problem is that it is counterproductive. It's during times like those that you should pause, take a deep breath, reflect, and say, "Yeah, but is he good to you and your Mom?" Or with the latter statement, "Well, not everyone can cook. The question is, does she treat you well?"

It is important for you to provide a neutral forum in which your children know they can come and talk openly. Don't take sides or jump on their bandwagon. If there are issues that need to be discussed, it should be done rationally and constructively with your ex-spouse.

If your children complain that you revealed private discussions with your ex-spouse, you should explain to them that the only reason you had a discussion with your ex-spouse was because you believed what they told you and it raised some concerns. Reinforce with them that *both* of you love them and will always try to protect them. Also let them know that in the future, if they say something that they want held in confidence, you will honor their wish, provided it does not place them in harm's way.

Notes and Thoughts

_____

_____

_____

_____

_____

_____

_____

_____

_____

_____

_____

14 | Doing That Blending Thing

(**Author's note:** *Okay, here's the deal. If you are not even close to getting married again or being interested in anybody, you have my permission to skip this chapter and to move on to the next one. But you have to promise me one thing. Keep this book in case you ever do think about getting married again, because there are some things in this chapter you will need to think about. It's a deal.*)

So, you were *never* getting married again, huh? Now you're thinking about it, or maybe you've already committed and are actually going to do it. I'll assume you're happy and excited about it, and since I know you're faithful to the principles of *The Parental Peace Accord*, I will also assume your children are accepting of it. So what does this mean?

Talk about a can of worms! This is an area that has so many variables that it's pretty hard to declare hard and fast guidelines. Because there are so many sets of human dynamics occurring all at the same time, it makes almost every situation case specific.

There is a reason we use the term *blended* when referring to the creation of a family that includes children from a previous marriage of at least one of the newlyweds. We have dynamics involving one parent and his or her children sharing their lives and living quarters with another adult and possibly his or her children. This blending can resemble the ease of coffee and cream or the difficulty of oil and water. Once again, it all starts with honesty and groundwork.

Certainly the process that this book endorses dictates that the children will have been allowed to express their feelings toward the matter and that those feelings have been given full consideration. Along with this is the assumption that you have determined that this marriage will not be detrimental to your children and, in fact, may be in their best interest. But that's the easy part. The initial decision is only the prelude to the day-to-day challenges that can be anticipated in this new living arrangement.

If you have decided to remarry, I think it is also important to consider what the relationship will be between your new spouse and your children. Will this person be a trusted friend to your children, or will this person assume a parental role? Again, there are hundreds of different circumstances that can affect this decision. If your ex-spouse is involved in your children's lives, then your new spouse might assume the role of a trusted friend with your children, unless your children are so fond of this person that they allow him or her to assume an additional parental role.

The trusted friend role has its own set of issues. Will your new spouse have any authority over your children and if so, what are the boundaries of that authority? What is the response the first time your new spouse hears, "Oh yeah? Well, you're not my parent!" Your new husband may be very comfortable spending extended periods of time alone with your son, but will he feel just as comfortable with your teenage daughter? Your new wife may be able to connect with your daughter, but will she be able to build a relationship with your son?

These are issues that should be discussed by *everybody* before that "I do" is declared for the second time. You and your new spouse had better be on the same page when it comes to parenting issues. If you're not, there will be full-time turmoil in your new family.

I recall a time when a stepfather was having a discussion with his stepdaughter regarding the continuous extreme filth and messiness of her room. He was very calmly explaining to her that the condition of her room was a reflection on her and could be considered a statement about her responsibility and self-esteem. In the middle of this conversation, the mother walked into the room and remarked, "For God's sake, clean your room so we don't have to listen to him."

This is an obvious example of a parent and stepparent who were not on the same wavelength when it came to the children. Aside from the tension this can create between the married couple, it sends very mixed messages to your children. On one hand the children are to respect your new spouse; however, on the other hand it doesn't seem to matter what the new spouse thinks about anything. If you put your children first, this isn't going to happen.

Avoiding these kinds of issues can be achieved through open dialogue between you, your new spouse, and your children. There needs to be an agreement as to what is expected of all parties. What can your children reasonably expect from your new spouse? What can your new spouse reasonably expect from your children? What kind of support can your new spouse expect from you? These are not easy questions, but it is imperative that they be addressed and agreed upon *before* you remarry. If this can't be done, you may be putting yourself and your children in a situation you will regret later.

The plot thickens if your new spouse is also bringing children into the marriage. These children may have been operating under a different set of rules than the ones that you and your ex-spouse set for your children. Whose set of rules prevail? And for those children who have been living under the non-prevailing parent's rules, just how confusing would that be? And what happens if you get along with your new spouse's children and your new spouse gets along with your children, but the children can't stand each other?

If you hope to be successful, I strongly suggest moving slowly. You must allow a lot of time for relationships to develop. Your kids need time to feel comfortable with this new person in your life. The children of this new person in your life need time to feel comfortable with you. None of this is going to happen overnight. If you and your new spouse are foolish enough to rush this process just so you can be together all the time, you risk living a life of hell for you and your children. Your children deserve better.

If your children are babies or preschoolers and your ex-spouse does not participate in their lives, it is certainly reasonable to assume that your new spouse could take on a parental role in raising your children. That raises another set of questions. Do you share the same parenting philosophies? Do you subscribe to time-outs or corporal punishment? Do you permit dating at fifteen, sixteen, or eighteen? Is curfew at 10:00 pm or 11:00 pm?

It is imperative that you both agree on discipline, manners, morals, and expectations in this blended environment. If you thought marriage was stressful the first time around, wait until you try it a second time with someone else's children. Again, love, honesty, and a lot of groundwork can go a long way in making this a happy and rewarding life. You just have to remember to put the children first and do what is in their best interest. They have to be the focus, not you.

More Than The Immediate Family

There is another set of issues that you will be addressing in a blended family arrangement. When we refer to blended families, we're not just talking about immediate family members. Many times there is a complete extended family that you must work with as well. Let's see, on your side of the family there are your parents, your ex-spouse's parents, your brothers and sisters, your ex-spouse's brothers and sisters, their children (your children's cousins), and possibly your aunts, uncles, and grandparents. Wow! Now double that for your new spouse's side of the family. And you thought family holidays were challenging *before*!

So let's talk about those family holidays. Certainly, there are some parents who take the attitude, "This is just way too much to deal with. Whoever wants to see us can come here." The problem is that is not exactly fair to your children *or* to your extended family. Part of childhood memories is getting together with family members during times of celebration. Your children may very well enjoy seeing their cousins, grandparents, and crazy Uncle Bob during the holiday season. Just as important, your family still loves your children and wants to be a part of their lives.

It is extremely painful to see how many grandparents are left out when divorce and blending occur. Grandchildren are the apples of their grandparents' eyes, and grandparents have looked forward to the time when they could spoil their grandkids without having to deal with the consequences. Likewise, many children think their grandparents are "really cool," and others consider them close friends who are always there for them and who never sit in judgment. If you are truly putting the best interest of your children first, you will work very hard to allow them the opportunity to enjoy strong family ties.

A Painful Confession

Okay, here's my big confession. I tried the blended family thing and it didn't work. Do you want to know why? Because I wasn't smart enough or insightful enough to do the exact things I am telling you to do in this chapter. Instead, I was all starry-eyed over this new woman in my life and pretty oblivious to everything around me—including the warning signs. I overlooked the fact that my new spouse-to-be never really took a sincere interest in my sons. Instead of seeing it as a warning sign, I thought it was flattering that my spouse-to-be preferred being with me when the children weren't around. And I was too blind to recognize the less-than-happy reactions of my sons to my marriage announcement.

I made the mistakes that many parents make in that situation; I made excuses and justified things I shouldn't have. For example, when my new spouse would wash her daughter's clothes, but refuse to wash my sons, I would explain to my sons that I wanted to teach them to do their laundry so they could be more responsible. In other words, I was covering up a situation because I didn't want them to feel as though their stepmother wasn't interested in them. This was not in the best interest of my children.

You know the rest of the story, and I don't have to go into details or give additional ugly examples of my stupidity. It didn't work and the marriage was short-lived. It wasn't because there were any bad people involved. This woman is a wonderful, hardworking, single mother, and we continue to have a friendly, cordial relationship. Her daughter and I remain friends, and she made a point of coming to my house on prom night so that I could see how great she looked. My sons are wonderful and although they are not perfect, they make good grades and pick the right friends. So this failure wasn't about bad people, it was about bad planning.

It didn't work because my priorities were wrong and our children weren't put first in the equation. It didn't work because the relationship was rushed in the scheme of things which didn't allow children and stepparent relationships adequate time to develop. It didn't work because there wasn't a meeting of the minds to establish understandings and expectations of everyone involved. It didn't work because we made it about us, not the children.

If you haven't learned anything else from my confession, at least understand that everybody, including you, will make mistakes. When this happens, you have two choices: One, you can beat yourself up forever and never forgive yourself; or two, you can take it and turn it into a positive. I chose the latter. Remember in the beginning of Chapter Ten how we talked about how all progress begins by telling the truth? Well, that's what I did.

First, after my wounds had healed, I took a long look at what had transpired and what role everybody had played. Then I took a critical look at the areas in which *I* had to accept responsibility. Second, I acknowledged the painful truth about what had happened. This required me to have an open an honest discussion with my sons. Lastly, I decided to include the painful experiences in this book in an effort to help others avoid the same pitfalls and to recount the consequences firsthand of what happens when you don't.

I'm happy to report that all progress *does* begin by telling the truth. My sons and I continue to have an incredible relationship, and I've stopped beating myself up for making the same mistakes that many before me have made. One positive result of this ordeal is that you are reading this chapter, and if you will just trust me and do what is being suggested as a part of *The Parental Peace Accord*, you can avoid a lot of stress and heartache for you and your children.

The Family Meeting

So now let's say you've been good students, done everything suggested, and you're still experiencing stress and having issues in your blended-family environment. Don't despair; the good news is that if prior to the relationship, you followed the blended-family suggestions, you have won half the battle. Because you followed the guidelines in this chapter, there was a mutual understanding of expectations before you all moved in together.

Now you are experiencing unbearable stress and issues, and that usually indicates that certain expectations are not being met. It's time for "The Family Meeting." This isn't a family meeting like you see in a National Lampoon movie. This is a meeting set in the same context as the meeting of the minds before the blended relationship began. Begin the meeting with a positive focus that recognizes what *is* working. Next, reflect back on what each person's expectations were in the beginning. Lastly, identify where each of you *feel* those expectations are not being met and why.

For the family meeting to work, certain ground rules must be established. Guns and knives must be checked at the door. A constructive, positive attitude needs to be maintained, so you might have to play facilitator. Everyone has to be given an equal opportunity to be heard without interruption. No name-calling allowed. Any criticism must be given in a constructive manner. If you feel like jumping down somebody's throat, instead say, "Help me understand where you're coming from on this."

Perhaps you're still saying I live in la-la land and that this will never work. You're right. It definitely will not work if you didn't follow these guidelines prior to entering into a blended-family environment. If you didn't have these kinds of discussions prior to the relationship, it is going to be unfamiliar territory for everyone now and has a slim chance of success. Conversely, if everyone entered into the blended family with a meeting of the minds and clear expectations, they have a reference point from which to start the family meeting.

So you see, we're back to that point about putting the children first, doing groundwork, and discussing expectations. A lot of work? Yes. But if you stop to consider how important your children are to you, and how stressful a dysfunctional family environment can be, it makes it very worthwhile. In fact, knowing what you know now and knowing what I've learned, you would be crazy not to engage in this hybrid form of "family planning."

It Can Work

I want to finish this chapter with some great news. There is an incredible number of happy, well-adjusted blended families out there. And for each one that is a success story, there are children who have received enormous benefits.

A close friend and business partner of mine married his wife when she was a single mother of babies. Her children's biological father never bothered to be a part of their lives. As a result, those children grew up only knowing only one father, their stepfather. Interestingly enough, they never considered him a stepfather. This is one of those blended families that has been extremely successful for the parents, but more importantly, for their children. I admire this couple greatly.

In Chapter Four, I referred to a very dear friend who had been married to an alcoholic who took no involvement in their children's lives. She remarried, and her three daughters developed such a deep love and affection for their stepfather that they actually considered him their father. They saw that he treated their mother and them with love and respect. This is certainly another successful blended family.

But the important thing is what that successful blending provided. It gave the girls father-daughter relationships, which would have otherwise been missing in their lives. It provided them with fond memories and a role model from which to raise their own children. Unfortunately, their stepfather recently passed away. When I went to the funeral home I was impressed by the deep love and admiration those three women had for this man. There was no question in anyone's mind that these girls were his daughters.

My last reflection involves a man I represented in a divorce. He and his wife had two beautiful little boys. Unfortunately, the wife felt the grass was greener on the other side of the fence and moved out of state, leaving her husband and two boys. My client, whom I'll call John, worked admirably at being a father, mother figure, provider, cook, housecleaner, and coach. He is truly one of my heroes.

About three years after his divorce, he met a delightful young woman at church who was also divorced. They dated for several years. She was unable to have children, and over the years, she developed a strong bond with the two young boys. Although they weren't living together, they would go on vacations together, spend holidays together, and attend the various activities of the boys together.

One day, when he least expected it, his sons came to him and announced, "Dad, we want Barbara to be our Mom." Although he hadn't expected it, he wasn't surprised. The dynamics of their relationships had developed in such a way that it became a natural course of events. To this day, they are a very happy family, and the boys have mother-son relationships that would not have existed had it not been for the successful blending.

Now I'm not suggesting that the kids do the family planning. However, I think this scenario shows how things can work out when the kids are put first. John and Barbara truly enjoyed being with John's sons and being involved in their activities. It became an integral part of their relationship. They didn't rush toward marriage. Life and relationships were allowed to run their natural courses without time being an issue. As a result, their blended family wasn't just about John and Barbara; it was also about the kids.

As you can see, even when you are considering re-entering the marital waters, the principles of *The Parental Peace Accord* apply more than ever. Second marriages are far from uncommon, even though few reports show them having a higher success rate than first marriages. But think about this; when you got married the first time it was easy. There were no children, you probably didn't have a lot of money, and all you had to concern yourself with was you and your fiancé.

It's different now. The second time around it is not just you and your fiancé. There are children involved who have the right to happy childhoods and to feel loved. You brought them into the world, you got divorced, and you have a responsibility to them. Sure, you may say, "Well, I deserve to be happy too, and if I'm not, how will my children be happy?" Like President Ronald Reagan used to say, "There you go again…"

Yes, you deserve to be happy. The point is that it is not just about you. If you focus only on your happiness without regard for the feelings of your children, then you are doing them a great disservice. "But wait," you argue, "my children won't always be here. I have to have a life." Right again, but the fact is they are here now and you have a responsibility to them now.

If you feel that you can't have a life until your children have left the nest, shame on you. First of all, there can be life without remarriage. Second, quit focusing on a self-serving marriage and focus on building the relationship. Lastly, quit feeling sorry for yourself and enjoy the moment. *Carpe diem!* Seize the day! Utilize a positive focus on building your new relationship and savor what you have. There are always those who would trade places with you in a heartbeat. The worse thing you can do for yourself, your significant other, and your children, is to force a marriage. Keep the priorities straight by putting the children first, and let nature take its course.

Notes and Thoughts

_____

_____

_____

_____

_____

15 | THE BEGINNING

Well, there you have it. In all likelihood, I have totally confused you, bored you, or given you just enough information to be dangerous. In a rather short period of time we have discussed a lot of important issues affecting your children. Since it didn't take you that long to read this book, I have a suggestion. In about two months, read this book again. I promise there will be some things that will hit you a little differently later.

Now you will notice that I called this last chapter "The Beginning." That's because reading this book was the easy part. Trying to actively participate in the principles of *The Parental Peace Accord* with your parenting partner for the benefit of your children is the hard part. The real work starts now. So if this chapter represents the beginning, where do you begin? I suggest the first thing you do is take a deep, cleansing breath and reflect on what has been discussed.

The unique process for creating your own specific parental peace accord consists of fifteen specific steps. They are all discussed in this book. For a future point of reference let's summarize each of these steps and give them a name for recognition. Additionally, for your convenience, each step is numbered to correspond to the chapter in which it was discussed. Pretty neat how that works, huh?

1. The Ultimate Commitment

In the introduction of this book I challenged you to show how much you love your children by committing to do uncomfortable and difficult things. Really unnatural things, like getting along with your ex-spouse. If most parents are willing to give their life for their children, having a civil relationship with the other parents seems like a small price to pay for your child's happiness. When you and your ex-spouse put the children first and make all decisions based on what is in their best interest, answers come a lot easier and make a lot more sense. Making it about the children is the foundation of *The Parental Peace Accord*.

2. The Healthy Perspective

I have also asked you to put things into perspective and not be too hard on yourself. Yes, the fact that you are getting a divorce places an emotional strain on your children. And yes, you may not be feeling very good about yourself right now. But if the marriage is over and the divorce was inevitable, then beating up on yourself is going to be nonproductive and time-consuming. Sorry, but there is just too much to be done for you to be wasting time. Life is short and you have a responsibility to your children, so get with it.

If you're staying in your marriage for your children, you are probably in denial. Kids aren't stupid. They usually know what's going on. Parents who have stayed in bad marriages for the sake of their children have usually subjected those children to stress, a less than favorable role model of what marriage is, and in the worst cases, abuse. Your children are entitled to feel loved and have a happy childhood and a positive environment. Give it to them.

3. The Correct Message

It's going to hurt when you break the news to your children that their parents are getting divorced. I'm talking about how it's going to hurt them, not you. If you're committed to doing it right, both parents need to be there. This shows your children you both care, and it eliminates the assumption that the absent parent is the "bad" person.

What you say to the children at this time is critical. To a large extent, your children's ages will dictate the approach you take in breaking this news. Children have different levels of emotional maturity

155

and understanding at different ages. The youngsters will need to be reassured that Mommy and Daddy still love them and will be there for them. The teenagers will need to be talked to as adults with open and honest dialogue. They may not show the emotions that a younger child might display, but you have still just turned their world upside down. They need you to be there for them, even if they don't admit it.

Timing is everything. I strongly suggest this news be delivered to your children on a weekend morning so that you are able to be with them and monitor their emotions. This is not something to lay on them right before they go to bed or get on the school bus. Suffice it to say, the best place for this discussion is probably at home. Let's not do the lunch-in-a-public-place scenario. That has a tendency to stifle and mask the true emotions that need to be expressed.

Every child will have a different reaction to the news of dissolution. Some will cry, some will withdraw, some will be angry, and some will even be happy. Your job is to know how to read your children and monitor those emotions. Be there for them and know whether they need to talk, have time to themselves, or be with their friends. Usually their biggest concern is the assurance that both parents still love them and will continue to be in their lives.

4. The High Road

There comes a time when parents must "seal thy lips." And that time is when you feel the urge to bad-mouth your children's other parent. In all likelihood, your children still loves this other parent, and your attempt to degrade that person will only backfire. In fact, when it is possible to do so, it will always serve you well to verbally acknowledge the good things about your ex-spouse. If the other parent really is a bad person, let your children figure that out, and they will. The comments you make will be more of a reflection on your character than that of your ex-spouse's. When discussing your children's other parent, the best advice is to take the high road.

5. The Negotiating Table

The entire relationship between you and your ex-spouse in participating in *The Parental Peace Accord* is based upon a series of negotiations. Some are simple and some are complex. There is a difference between negotiating in the best interest of your children and arguing. It's not about winning; it's about doing what is best for the children. You and your parenting partner should make an effort to decide everything you can between yourselves. As parents, you should be in a better position to know what is best for your children than a stranger in a black robe.

It is also important to remember that while children don't belong at the negotiating table, you certainly want to consider their input in determining what is best for them. All negotiations should be between you and your parenting partner. This is especially true in money matters. Even teenage children really don't have a good grasp on financial issues.

6. The Best Custody

There are several forms of custody that jurisdictions recognize. Of all the issues to consider throughout your dissolution, custody is the one for which it is most important to remember it is about the children, not you. Too many parents concern themselves with what other people will think in terms of custody rather than focusing on what is best for their children.

The best custody arrangement depends on a number of factors which include, but are not limited to the following: age, gender, parents' work schedules, geographic locations, the children's interests, and characters of the parents. Once again, if anybody should know the children well enough to make the best decisions on their behalves it should be their parents. But if parents can't come to an agreement on this issue, a judge will decide what is in the best interest of their children.

Child support payments should not be a determining factor when parents are considering custody. Those who base custody preferences on child support have their priorities all mixed up. Most jurisdictions use schedules or formulas to determine support payments. If custody is not agreed upon by the parents, the court will make the custody determination before it will even consider child support.

7. The Valuable Visitation

Visitations with the non-custodial parent is provided to allow the child and parent the opportunity to have quality, uninterrupted time in an effort to maintain and develop a balanced relationship. Although most jurisdictions refer to non-custodial parents' visitation rights, the visitation is designed to serve the best interest of the children. This creates an issue as to whether or not visitation is an obligation to be fulfilled or a right that may or may not be exercised.

Those parents committed to *The Parental Peace Accord* will not have this issue because the non-custodial parents will want to spend as much time as possible with the children because it is in the best interest of the children for both parents to be very involved in their lives. Visitation time is a valuable bonding opportunity that creates stability and security for the children. If parents can't agree on visitation, the court will issue a visitation schedule that it has adopted. Typically a court is not going to hold parents accountable for following the guidelines if they have mutually agreed on other arrangements.

An easy way to avoid pick-up problems with visitation is to agree that the person receiving the children is responsible for picking the children up. In other words, if Dad is exercising visitation he would pick the children up. When his visitation is over, Mom will pick the children up. This prevents a lot of confusion and awkwardness from standing outside an unanswered door or sitting in a parking lot somewhere.

Most importantly, the parent exercising visitation should focus on quality time with the children. This doesn't mean trying to see how many activities you can pack into one fun-filled weekend. It means having fun with your children and enjoying each other's company. Your child is going to be a lot more interested in getting to spend quality time with you, rather than what it is the two of you are going to do or how much money you're going to spend. Take time to talk and *listen* to your children. Find out what's going on in their lives. Let them know you're interested.

8. The Avoidance of Abuse

This is an area of zero-tolerance. Children are entitled to carefree happy childhoods filled with fun memories. There is *never* justification for abusing children. The ramifications and consequences of physical and sexual abuse are pretty obvious. But parents who neglect or reject their children are subjecting them to psychological abuse.

It is just as damaging when parents don't allow their children to have pictures of their other parents, don't allow phone calls, or prohibit contact with the other parent for no reason. This type of emotional abuse will be long remembered by your children. Similarly, parents who play mind games with their children also take unfair advantage of a children's vulnerability.

The parents who finds themselves engaging in this conduct should reflect on how they would feel if the other parent were using psychological warfare to turn their children against them. The point is very simple; it is damaging and not in the best interest of your children. The point is it's abusive; stop it!

9. The Routine

During the turmoil and uncertainty that is created during a divorce, children are in dire need of some certainty and stability in their lives. Contrary to a first blush reaction to the term, routines are good. Routines and traditions are powerful ways to provide your children with stability and security. Routines create expectations that are usually met. The routines can be something as simple as a bedtime, going to church, a curfew, or discipline. A good place to start is to look at the things that were routine before the divorce and attempt to keep as many of those rituals in place as possible.

Routine activities can also be special times. Maybe it's that annual trip to the beach, Christmas at Grandma's, or that post-game pizza.

Conversely, some routines are behind the scenes and play an important part in creating stability. For instance, it is important for parents to routinely exchange information with each other regarding school work, medical reports, practice schedules, and anything else that would help each of them stay "in the loop" as to what is going on in their children's lives.

Most importantly, when it comes to routines, the small ones are just as powerful as the big ones when it comes to creating a stable environment for your children. Remember my example of how my sons always sat in the same chairs at the kitchen table, and how to this day, they continue to do so when they come home! These day-to-day, subconsciously performed activities and habits are all part of the foundation of a stable environment, and this environment is what makes your children feel secure. Your job is to recognize these things and facilitate their recurrence.

10. The Honesty Policy

Even members of Alcoholics Anonymous know that all progress begins by telling the truth. The same principle applies in the dissolution environment. It will not serve your children well if you are in a state of denial regarding your divorce. Until you recognize and openly admit to yourself that "I am a divorced parent," there can be no forward movement.

Honesty with your children will go a long way in helping them adjust to the new circumstances of their lives. Parents shouldn't use their children as counselors or emotional crutches, but it's okay to share honest feelings with them. If your child is questioning your mood, you can be honest and tell her, "Oh, just one of those days. I guess I've got the blues." You won't appear weak to your child if you tell him or her, "Oh, I don't know; I'm just feeling a little insecure today."

This kind of honesty not only lets your children realize that you're human, but it makes it easier for them to be honest and share their feelings with you. Be honest with them about the positive things too. Let them know that guy at the office asked you out to dinner. Let them know how much you love them. Let them know how lucky you feel to be their parent.

11. The Right Stuff

If *The Parental Peace Accord* is going to work, there will be times when you will have to set your emotions aside and force yourself to do the right thing. This step is the most powerful in having a successful working relationship with your parenting partner. It requires you to go above and beyond what is expected. It may be something as simple as giving your children money so they can buy their other parent a Christmas gift. They want to be able to give presents like everybody else. If you really want to surprise your ex, offer to watch the kids when she needs to get away, even if it is for a date. This all may sound far-fetched to you, but remember you're doing this because it is best for the kids. Who would they benefit being with more, a baby-sitter or you?

Now it is very possible that your ex-spouse will not reciprocate. Don't dwell on that. He or she may come around eventually. In the meantime, you have set a great example for your children, and they will remember you always took the high road.

12. The Expectations

It is amazing how much our emotions are influenced by our expectations. If we have an expectation and it doesn't happen, we will often feel frustrated or even angry. If we expect something good to happen, and it does, then we are pleased that our expectation was met. Recognizing expectations and their effects can alleviate a great deal of stress in your life. I used the example that I was be upset because my son didn't bring in the empty trash cans from the end of the driveway. In truth, I wasn't really that upset about the trash cans; I was upset because my expectation of him to bring them in was not met. In the scheme of things it wasn't that big of a deal, but the expectation was very real.

Likewise, our children will have certain expectations. It is important to help them determine whether those expectations are realistic. We can also help them prepare for the possibility that a certain expectation may not be met. Help them understand how powerful expectations are in affecting our emotions.

The expectations are everywhere. Our children expected us to be married forever. In determining college education obligations, the courts will look at what may have been reasonable expectations if the marriage had not failed. We expect our parenting partner to be on time when exercising visitation.

Here's a question for you. What are your children's expectations? If you don't know, then you need to ask. There are non-intrusive ways to do this, some of which we discussed in Chapter Twelve. It is important to know our children's expectations because it will help us prepare them for the emotional outcomes.

13. The Stranger

Introducing a new person into your children's lives is tricky at best. If the groundwork hasn't been laid for this introduction, a thousand questions will be swimming in your children's heads. Who is this person? How serious is this relationship? Are they going to get married? Will I have to call her Mom? What if he/she doesn't like me?

The best way to prepare for this is open and honest communication from the very beginning. "This cute guy at work asked me out. What do you think I should do?" Your approach is going to be governed by a lot of factors, such as the age of your children, how long you've been divorced, and how you met this new person, just to name a few. If this "new" person is someone you were seeing during your marriage and your children know it, it may be pretty difficult to get their acceptance.

It is important for this new person to know that they only get to make a first impression once. They need to be sincere and honest. It is important that the children see them for who they really are. If they come on too strong, the children are going to think the person is a flake. If they are too reserved, the children are going to think they have the personality of a doorknob or that the they don't like them. The bottom line is this: if it doesn't work for your kids, then it's not going to work.

14. The Blend

It's not uncommon for divorced parents to say "I will *never* get married again." But they do. When that happens, one of the most complex set of human dynamics is created. We refer to it as a "blended" family because it is a mixture of children, parents, stepchildren, and stepparents. Once again, this will only work if the adult parties put the children first.

In putting the children first you have to know what they are feeling. If you have gone about the relationship wisely, the children will probably be comfortable with this new living arrangement. But if you are rushing this so that you and your new love can be together, you run the risk that the children aren't ready. If that's the case, you shouldn't do it. Even when it is painful, if the children are still your responsibility (meaning they are not emancipated), they come first, and you shouldn't get remarried.

I realize I probably seem harsh here, but most couples go into blended family arrangements and are clueless as to what it will entail. If both parties are bringing children into the marriage, how do the children get along? Do they even like each other? And which child gets which bedroom, and why? And which set of discipline rules do we use, and why? And what about the extended family of both sides?

Am I saying blended families can't work? Absolutely not! There are countless blended families that have not only made it work, but provided children with positive results that they would not have experienced otherwise. Many times second-marriage spouses have stepped in for a biological parent who took no part in the children's lives, and the children became benefactors of a warm family relationship. I'm only saying that there is a lot of planning and work involved. Everybody better be on the same page, and there are a lot of pages in the blended family environment.

15. The Follow-Through

So now you are in a position to determine whether you have what it takes to participate in *The Parental Peace Accord*. It really is a lot more work than you think. It will require some emotional stamina that you didn't know you had. There will be times when your ex-spouse is uncooperative or obstinate, and it would be easy to let the emotions take over and fire away. However, this can be avoided.

Here's the secret: your kids. If you stop to think about how much you care for them and how important it is that a divorce doesn't prevent them from having balanced, happy childhoods, you'll find the strength to make *The Parental Peace Accord* work for you.

You see, I wrote this book for your kids. I don't mean just any kids; I mean *your* kids. They didn't have any say or choice in your decision to get a divorce. They are the product of a marriage that didn't work. But I am determined to show that this doesn't mean they have to be victims. I'm determined to ensure that you will do everything in your power to let them have happy childhoods and feel loved. I can't think of a better epitaph for someone than one that declares, "He was a good father," or "She was a good mother." I want you to be that good parent. I want you and your children to have a happy and well-adjusted life together.

Now, I've got you started, but you have to follow through. Yes, you know what comes next—- Step One. You have to sit down with your parenting partner and have that heart-to-heart about what is important. It's a difficult step, but it will make your life so much easier if you are successful. You must be successful. It's a little like the chief of NASA Ground Control telling his staff when Apollo 13 was in danger of not returning to earth: "Failure is not an option!"

Go visit your ex. Don't think of him or her as your ex-spouse. Think of your ex as a parent and your parenting partner. Get them to read this book. Read it again yourself. Then keep referring back to it to see if you are staying the course. Some people need a written commitment to take on a task like this. For those, I have prepared a sample version of a parental peace accord so that they don't get bogged down. Feel free to write your own. Just get started on this. Your children are waiting.

And that is what you must always remember. It's about the children; not you.

Notes and Thoughts

_____

_____

_____

_____

_____

_____

_____

_____

_____

_____

_____

_____

_____

_____

_____

_____

_____

_____

_____

_____

_____

_____

_____

APPENDIX

The Parental Peace Accord:

*Come now the undersigned, as parents with a deep and abiding love for **our children**, and for their best interest, do hereby agree as follows:*

1. *To always cooperate and communicate as parenting partners, put **our children** first, and make all decisions based on what is in their best interest.*
2. *To view each other as parents, rather than ex-spouses, in an effort to maintain a healthy perspective for the benefit of **our children**.*
3. *To jointly deliver difficult news (such as our divorce) to **our children** in such a way that it is best for them and provides them with the most support.*
4. *To refrain from speaking or referring negatively about each other in the presence of **our children** and remembering that we are each parents whom **our children** love.*
5. *To keep all negotiations between us and to never place **our children** in the middle of those negotiations.*
6. *To agree to a custody arrangement that is in the very best interest of **our children**, without regard to our own convenience or what others might think.*
7. *To exercise and allow liberal and flexible visitation that allows **our children** to have happy, fulfilling relationships and to bond with both parents.*
8. *To avoid and prevent any abuse of any form to **our children** and to treat them with the respect they deserve.*

9. To provide **our children** with stability and security by utilizing routines and traditions for the benefit of **our children**.

10. To always be honest with each other and **our children** and to engage in honest conversations with **our children** to provide them with emotional security.

11. To always do the right thing for each other and for **our children**, above and beyond what may be expected.

12. To identify, acknowledge and discuss expectations of each other and of **our children** in an effort to avoid unmet expectations.

13. To introduce any new relationships to **our children** in an honest, open, and forthright manner to allow **our children** an opportunity to adjust and accept.

14. To put **our children** and their best interests first through open discussions when considering any relationship that would require a "blending" of living arrangements.

15. To continually follow through, monitor, and communicate the principles that this Parental Peace Accord represents in an effort to provide **our children** with a continuous, happy, and secure childhood.

We enter into The Parental Peace Accord on this _____day of __ _____, _____ as a commitment and acknowledgement that it is about **our children**, not us.

_____   _____
Father   Mother

ABOUT THE AUTHOR

Jack Bailey was born in Zurich, Switzerland. He has never met his birth parents, and prior to his first birthday, a U.S. soldier made arrangements for him to be brought to the United States. A few years later he became a ward of the California Department of Social Services. At the age of ten he was on an airplane destined for Indianapolis, to live with people he didn't know in a place he had never been. He carried all of his belongings in a single brown paper grocery sack. When he was twelve years old he was naturalized as a U.S. citizen and had his name officially changed to Jack Bailey.

He received a bachelor's degree in Communications from Indiana University. Later he also received his law degree from Indiana University and was sworn in as a member of the Indiana State Bar in 1984. The majority of his practice has been in the area of family law, business law, and litigation. At the time this book was written, he was the President of the Johnson County Bar Association in Indiana. He is also certified as a Civil and Family Law Mediator.

As a highly regarded speaker, counselor, businessman, and mediator, he is known for his no-nonsense approach seasoned with humorous observations of life around us. His wisdom, sense of humor, sincerity, and passion have endeared him to clients and audiences around the world. His joy in life is spending time with his two sons, who are both currently enrolled at his alma mater, Indiana University.